Emily D. and You and Me

Emily D. and You and Me

Women Reflect on Identity, Trauma,
Housekeeping, Death, Gardens, and Awakening

ELLEN HARRINGTON

RESOURCE *Publications* • Eugene, Oregon

EMILY D. AND YOU AND ME
Women Reflect on Identity, Trauma, Housekeeping, Death, Gardens, and
Awakening

Resource Publications
An Imprint of Wipf and Stock Publishers
199 W. 8th Ave., Suite 3
Eugene, OR 97401

www.wipfandstock.com

PAPERBACK ISBN: 978-1-6667-1920-8
HARDCOVER ISBN: 978-1-6667-1921-5
EBOOK ISBN: 978-1-6667-1922-2

08/25/21

With deep gratitude, to the bunch of you,
who are present for me from the earliest glimmers of the book,
whether you know it or not.

Julia Bergstrom
Joanie Delamater
Margot Harrington
Katherine Kegan
Jane Keyes
Michael Lapsley
Marilyn Moore
Sar and Jer Harrington Smith
Indi and Heidi Smith
Kay Vander Voort
Frank Wilson

and a later group that offered insight and support

Patty Wheeler Andrews
Judy Benham
Scott Edelstein
Sharon Hamilton
Deborah Keenan
Jean Larson
Isabel Legarda
Lawrence Sutin

and, of course, Emily Dickinson

the unexamined life is not worth living.

—Socrates

I know not but the next
would be my final inch—
This gave me that precarious Gait
Some call Experience.

—Emily Dickinson

December 3, 2005

No portents hissed as my hand picked a card from the drugstore rack. I was in ordinary, lawful pursuit of a sympathy message. An innocent objective. Among the choices was a little black quatrain whose words looked handwritten. The words were pushed into prominence by the pallid watercolor wash behind. I read the lines and noted that they were by Emily Dickinson. The little quatrain ran, "This world is not conclusion . . . a species stands beyond—invisible as music—as positive as sound . . ." The startling clarity of those four lines beguiled me as surely as a compass points north. And after my initial gasp, I did not feel a bit presumptuous as I laid claim to a mutual understanding. As if we each knew William Blake moments where spaciousness opens in a grain of sand or a sunbeam dancing with dust motes. An eyeful of infinity. I absorbed her perfect pitch about the proximity and reality of the eternal.

I bought the card. Filled its inner blankness with a few lines of my own. And recorded Emily's lines in a journal to keep them handy. I was certain to want them again. Fortunately only a few times since, but they never fail to bring me into the neighborhood of Otherness. I hope as much for the one receiving condolence.

The card piqued my curiosity about Emily Dickinson. It inspired me to learn more. I bought the Thomas H. Johnson edition of *The Complete Poetry of Emily Dickinson*. I fell into it again and again—to find ripe fruits of resonance on every page. She knew what I know about the bite and laugh of language, the color and creep of seasons, and the drag of thought-forms such as class, race, and patriarchy. She knew the adventure of hewing a word path through misty thickets of inherited culture to find restful meadows where adaptive byways might be attempted. Gradually, Emily revealed herself as my alter ego. A kindred spirit.

At the time I bought the card, I shared the conventional lore of Emily Dickinson. I knew what everyone knew. She is a notable American poet, an urban legend of her era in that not much fact can be verified amid speculation about her love life and eccentricity. She tried publishing her poems but an editor protecting the prevalent, sweetly pastoral literary turf, did not encourage her effort. She lived in Amherst, Massachusetts, an 1800s hotbed of alternative philosophy that was set apart by a belief in transcendent states perceived through intuition rather than the doctrine of established religion. She wore white sometimes which is curious since white in American culture is the symbolic preserve of wedding dresses and shrouds. And I know she never married. She was reclusive. Certainly not unusual for a single woman at that time. Kidney disease took her in early middle age.

As I read Emily's poetry, I began to write my own. About fifteen years ago, I spent a year writing poetry. Words fell out of my head . . . into the lines of a couple of hundred poems. Short and spare.

> Oh envy, Emily D.
> that I had time to be
> behind parlor screens
> absorbing words
> without demands
> requiring banalities

One memorable day, Emily visited. The preamble to her visit begins with my old habit of keeping a small figurine on my desk at work. I touched it when I felt adrift, when a wave, such as underemployment, surged. The figurine was a bear. It was cute for my usual taste but had a fair quotient of cuddle appeal attributed to bears.

I called it M, the name that came to me at point of purchase. I left work one sweltering day and walked across heat-softened asphalt to my car. As I walked, socked by hot after frigid air-conditioning, an image of the bear popped into my brain as if just the memory of it had the power to calm. It occurred to me that the bear's name was Emily. I opened the car door and paused to let the day's heat dissipate. When I leaned in to sit, I 'saw' a blur and knew that in the passenger seat was Emily looking just like the picture of her as a teenager. She 'said' to me, "I don't want this to happen to anyone else." As I got into the car, the blur faded, but my shabby old rattle-trap smelled like roses all the way home.

I have mulled over her comment for years. What was the 'this' that did she not want to happen to anyone else? Unrequited love? Patronizing editors? Or maybe she meant what Oliver Wendell Holmes meant when he wrote, "Alas, for those who never sing, but die with all their music in them."

More and more I identified with Emily. With our retreat into words—the life of the mind. With our mutual disgust over centuries of dismissiveness imposed upon women. With our confinement by cultural customs. With the conformity extracted by every tribe in every era. Few women have pushed back against these constraints, although Emily seems to have tried.

She chafed under the assumption that she would fulfill her feminine destiny without question. She refused to be part of the revivalist faith that controlled her family and friends. Her young tutor, Ben Newton, encouraged her writing but throughout her life, she sought mentors among older men who were articulate, reflective, and verbal. She sought those qualities in herself though they were the very ones most likely to prevent her from becoming a wife. Men wanted hardworking wives and mothers on the home front as their intellectual interests were met in those bastions of male conviviality—work and clubs. Her friends eventually married or moved away.

She had to make a life for herself in Amherst. Both Emily and I have been affected by the stereotype of a single woman in a man's world. Struggled with the implicit perception that there must be something wrong with a single woman. Emily had to choose between being a housewife or a spinster. Such a shriveled, forlorn word-combining a wheeze and a spit. Her father had to approve any prospective match. And he did not, more than once. As she got older and more opinionated, a marriage of equals proved evasive. She remained single rather than settle for a spouse who could not match wits with her own.

In forward-thinking circles of my generation, it is acceptable for women to be unmarried. Culture still presses for wives and mothers but in the 21st century, there is a genuine choice. Women can try for a balance between career and family to engage intellect and emotion. No such possibility for Emily. Soon after her death in 1886 came suffragettes and women making inroads in all professions.

We have helped each other leave behind dead stereotypes for broader options. A remaining hindrance is helping men find the interest and emotional nimbleness to keep up with their own role changes. Emily may have been more at home in the current era, although without the forerunner's angst to goad her, the piercing quality in her poetry might well have been muted to a softer stridency.

My own history in the repeating female script has been the subject of years of journal entries. I have a box the size of ten reams of paper that contains the scribbles of thirty-odd years. I have small books–spirals–leather–plain paper–colored paper–thick–thin–some filled in weeks, others spanned several years.

Occasionally, I am tempted to wait upon evolving thought or a new season before cracking blank pages. The possibilities of the next volume can seldom wait. Journals arrive and begin exactly as needed. Clippings and quotes of my own and others are written, taped, and stapled on the pages. My insight is stored alongside that of others who say what I know in my head but not yet in my experience. Much of my reflection shows a long, weary, and repetitive wander in a determined search of missing pieces of personhood.

Emily did not keep a journal as far as we know. She did write hundreds of letters. Many included poems and dried flowers. Collections of her letters are similar to modern journals that have replaced letter writing. We write to ourselves about ourselves. Increasingly, personal connection is virtual and abbreviated to emojis as stand-ins for words or touch.

Four or five years ago, while I was typing away at some assignment, pummeling originality from my brain, a little thought skittered across my internal screen. I wondered what Emily would have written if she had kept a journal or a diary as the Victorians would have called such a record.

From that moment, I began to imagine an old book. In my mind's eye, it was discovered at the back of a closet or in the crannies of musty attic storage. I like old books. I like books period. Reading brings the enthralling thought of the best of friends at my bidding. I have long experienced writerly residue darting at me off the page like a disoriented bird. Remnants of their intent and feeling linger, leaving me to muddle with meaning. When in need of advice or comfort, my seemingly random bookcase selections seldom fail to amaze with their aptness.

While I like old books, other old things feel heavy to me. They exude a stuffy, coffinesque quality. Most are expensive to acquire and high maintenance thereafter. They burden inheritors, who would rather escape the obligations imposed by finishes to preserve, bindings to keep supple, and hand painting to hand wash.

Old things can bulge oppressively into the present. I prefer simple, clean lines designed by Scandinavians. Light wood lines that slice simply through their space. Concise, compact lines that pack multi-function into small spaces. Self-effacing lines that let eyes slide to objects placed on them.

Good fortune for me to live in a time when I can choose my style. Old and dark dust-catching eruptions of scrollwork and carving? Toe-cracking knobs on curvaceous legs? I think not. I pick lean, light shapes for low-maintenance living. Simplicity.

But call to mind an old manuscript. A journal compacted with letters and lines. Smell the throat-catching odor of old paper.

See frail, creamy pages covered with racing script. Even eyestrain induced by stiff, faded cursive would find me captive. Believe that this journal was left by Emily Dickinson.

As I imagined the journal, I wanted to read it cover to cover immediately. To look for clues about the meaning of the comment made to me in my car. In the journal's absence, I created a dialogue. Emily's side. My side. I wrote down the dialogue—my interpretation of her life while I rummaged around for hints to explain the comment.

I wrote as if I were Emily. Then replied from the middle of my life more than a century later. As you read the parallel journal entries, I hope you find something new to savor as you imagine how you might reply to each of us—what you would include in our dialogue.

For myself, I wanted to bring to light the locales where our lives, inner lives mainly, are alike. I expected a likeness. I wrote in search of eternal archetypes among women even when our physical lives across centuries bear little resemblance. This 'old' journal written on behalf of each of us is a multi-century account of our mutual determination to heed Holmes' warning and die with our music sung—fully choral, symphonic, rocked, and jazzed.

Emily herself has not deigned to make quite such a dramatic return. The initiative seems to originate from her side with the timing one would expect from invisible wisdom. An early going-back-to-college class found me in required attendance at a session on how to use the library for research. The instructor projected the computer images on a screen, entered a search word 'fruit' and the first reference that displayed was a book called *The Gardens of Emily Dickinson*. I nodded to the idea that there can be a surprising method in all things.

I have stopped expecting that I'll find Emily sitting at my kitchen table, though she has been invited. There was an occasion a few months ago when I did not 'see' her but most definitely 'felt' her nearby. I was at a poetry group meeting during which one of the members was telling us about a church choir that was setting Emily

Dickinson's poetry to music. This led me to make the inevitable, somewhat irreverent comment that any Emily poem could be sung to the tune of "The Yellow Rose of Texas" with its hymn-like meter. That is indeed the rhythm she used. I quietly intoned, 'hope is the thing with feathers . . . ' amid a flutter of chuckles. As we refocused on the poetry book, I brushed at one eye behind my glasses. I thought perhaps a hair had caught in my eyelashes. As I tried to find it—my fingers caught instead of a tiny, perfect white feather! My breath caught, the back of my neck tingled and a deep 'oh!' stayed silent in the midst of our discussion.

I kept the feather. Taped it in my journal. Once in a while, I revisit that moment of connection. Emily revealed a sense of humor as well as a validation that I am on the right track with 'our' journal. I am pursuing what she intended. When I need her particular presence, I open to a poem, find her on the page and feel her satisfaction with our words.

As an example, a few weeks ago, my second job disappeared. During a low day, I opened at random my pocket edition of selected Emily poems and read,

> ". . . I find my feet have further Goals—
> I smile upon the Aims
> That felt so ample—Yesterday—
> Today's—have vaster claims—
> I do not doubt the self I was
> Was competent to me—
> But something awkward in the fit—
> Proves that outgrown—I see—"

My intention is that Emily's part of the journal is a gift of solace to herself after many deaths, a nervous breakdown, and her first attack of kidney disease. I gave Emily a compulsion to write about her life. To signify what she called 'her circumference.' To let her write plainly to a world that never wrote back.

And my part of the journal shows many years of writing in the miasma of our lowest-common-denominator culture in search of our lost depth and the lost wonder of our glorious, but unrecognized individual value.

Emily D. and You and Me

historic places breathe
thought forms linger
an exhalation of continuity

April 16, 1884

WHAT IS THE COMMOTION BEATING ON MY SILENCE FROM
below? It sounds like a bear blundering about the rooms.
Ransacking the cupboards, maybe seeking sustenance. Sleep
is impossible amid the din. I am awake and feel more cheerful
today, although illness increases its hold and I do not escape its
grasp for long.

Memory has supplied commotion's cause. Spring-cleaning.
Winter's soot and dust are sent summarily out of doors. Sister
Vinnie and our faithful house help, Maggie, do the rooms over.
I am excused this year. I am meant to be resting to recover
my health. Truth be told, I would choose spring-cleaning over
illness. Headache and nausea drag themselves through my organs
without cease. Not overwhelming, but still unwilling to abandon
me quite yet. My hands feel fevered. Thank heaven for pen and
paper to relieve their hot fidgets. My penchant for keeping to
home magnifies when I have to keep to my room and bed.

Newborn mewls announced my arrival in the room across
the hall. Followed by my tottering attempts at verticality. My daily
moments of exhaustion deepen as I recall the hurry of childhood
up and down the stairs and in and out the doors to answer the
urgency of play.

Slimy toadstools of dishonor sprout if I mull over the history
of the family homestead. It was just home until Grandfather
Dickinson's injudicious use of funds became apparent. Father had
to sell half the house. We lived in one half, with the Mack family

moved into the other half. When this proved an insufficient step, Father sold our half which required us to decamp to a house out of town center on Pleasant street. After fifteen years of pleasant living, hand in hand with modest economies, finance, and availability allowed for the repurchase of our family property.

My child's memory made the rooms cavernous. An adult sense of scale prevailed once we returned. The rooms were adequate for function and aesthetics. Though space limitations sent the annual Amherst College graduation party hosted by Father and Mother into the garden.

Once re-established at the homestead, the Georgian regularity of home was interrupted by the ell Father added. The north arm gave us a new kitchen, a shed, and a washroom. The back door of the ell shielded the careless, low-born heraldry of the washing line. The short eastern arm became the dining room. Father seconded the old dining room for his library. A site of many furtive visits to see if any new and approved literature had arrived for perusal. The most important addition was the conservatory. My little garden off the dining room. Father ordered its construction. I wonder, did he know my need for green and growing things in all seasons, or did he hope that there was status in conservatory dirt under my fingernails? Just now I am too ill to tend my sunny haven. Vinnie has to prune, water, and coax according to my precise instructions.

When spring cleaning begins in earnest, we have our own bit of desert with dust from three staircases, two parlors, the dining room, and a roomful of books whose concave tops trap flecks in neat little runnels. We open all the windows. Fresh smelling spring pushes out stale, musty air granted house space over the winter.

The house takes heart right down to its foundation. The root cellar, its contents mostly consumed, suffers an infusion of light. Dust is discretely shuffled away.

The gummy tracery of webs removed. Resident insects are deprived of home. Perhaps we do them a favor by forcing them to begin anew. Maybe the most hiding spiders survive to search for new spots most advantageous for entrapment.

Vinnie's industry is commendable—sweeping away dry leaves and scrubbing patches of grime are useful antidotes to thoughts about the mystery of time and aging. She finds that realm fearful and turns to her work with the vigor of avoidance.

As I write, Vinnie and Maggie increase the commotion. The bear must have been joined by a doltish moose made to rake pictures off the walls with its antlers. Perhaps they could find a frantic deer to drag the rugs out for beating.

Spring-cleaning, with all due ritual, is being enacted. As often as we clean, the furniture and pictures might as well be mortared to the walls. Art, seating, and storage pieces stagger from their corners and leave imprints behind on paint and paper. The greasy outlines never completely disappear. Thus, items must return to hover around us from their original places.

The house is cleaner for a time, though essentially unchanged. In this circumference of home, ideas beg for admittance at the doorstep of my mind. If I allow them to enter—new considerations come into play and may stay to firmly usurp tired attitudes and conclusions. I am a changed person trying to accommodate the unchanged clime.

My unchanged clime leads to thoughts of childhood. It passed quickly and with many changes of thought and stature. It passed into an adulthood of days that differ little, one from another. When I seek childhood among the snowy hillocks of my sheets, it appears in my mind like a soft fog from which memory flashes like a lighthouse relieving my darkness and guiding me through danger. Circles of light move among memories. They shine on my history in a manner that lessens hurt lingering in rocky-edged memories that remind me of loss.

One such circle of memory is the closet. A grave-like space of brief confinement intended to teach me to be still. One could never begin too early to impose decorum. What I learned was to be my lively, curious self outside of Mother's sight and hearing. Her vague gentleness did not pry into my doings as long as they stayed beyond earshot and as long as I entertained and eased discourse with my wit.

I did so amid cooking lessons bestowed from Mother's renown in her well-regulated home. Although the college commencement, her worthy repast, sorely taxed her social talents. Literary endeavors were beyond her sphere. Even a letter to Austin, her beloved son, was too onerous a challenge.

Another circle of light glows around the small bedroom shared by Vinnie, me, and our brother Austin. We came separately from the same womb, only to spend years being a trio of sleepers in its imitation where we heard each others' breathing and felt the bumps of arms and legs stretching for space. Compacted into half a house, our exuberance found a more forgiving home outside. Our small fingers were pressed into service when we could be helpful. It was good preparation for adult duties. Mother was never not working. Her efforts more often than not hampered by three children fussing around her feet like mice.

Quiet as mice, certainly, when Father was at home. The exception being his occupation with his legal briefs, then our youthful occupations passed unnoticed. He did feel entitled to tranquility when at home, and indeed, when we all gathered in the space where heat and light were in generous supply, a quiet calm pervaded.

He strenuously dispensed energy into his law profession, his activities at the College, and the righteousness expected from a pillar of First Congregational church. Few civic projects in town were established without benefit of his approval. He was a man of conviction. He encouraged education, even for women, but also made it plain that different qualities were desirable in a female who entered domestic relations. The effect of this on my adult life was to deprive me of an occupation apart from breathing and automatic adherence to our habitual regime.

My Puritan antecedents bred hard work, duty, stamina, and thrift into the family bloodlines—just as they abounded among the staid citizenry of Amherst. I quibbled most persistently with their narrow practice that made no allowance for personal thought. The revivalist rhetoric that swept through varied not in its application. I learned that it was possible for a people to move lockstep through the days, dully unaware of consciousness plucking at their sleeves. I did not, could not really, choose to be a functionary. Instead, words and ideas formed into the sting of poetry that sliced through my skin from the inside—followed by a delicious shiver, like a self-healing wound, once the words were on the outside.

July 7, 1884

Awake with an itch to be active, even if it is just my fingers writing letters to myself. Ink etches enlightenment in mildly illegible arcs. I want to explore my circumference. My circumference—the marital matrix of my creation and the culture of family, community, and country that fostered my emergence— fostered my materialization as I became ever more conjoined to earthly universe of invisible holies. My circumference harmonizes the melody of people and circumstances around me. I left hints of its existence in poems. My version of 'knowings.'

Today I am mindful of the poems that bolstered and consumed me so. My older eyes are dispassionate. Had I a readership like George Eliot or Charles Dickens, a following anxiously awaiting new installments, I think few readers would have stuck with my word jungles long enough to enter their precepts. Just as Mr. Higginson of "Atlantic Monthly" did not enter when I sent him poetry to see if it breathed. It seemed that I could not even give it away—perhaps I should include a pound of tea!

But my publishing urges are not quite so black and white. My friend, Helen Hunt Jackson, acclaimed my work. She begged for new selections. She wrote to me, "It is a cruel wrong to your day and generation that will not give them light . . . I do not think we have a right to withhold from the world a word or thought any more than a deed, which might help a single soul." This jogged my conscience. I remembered a fainting robin. I

wonder if I have lived in vain—regret pinches that I did not
avail myself often of her cheer and support to ease my many
withholdings. As I leaf through my tenderly tied little packets
now, I perceive a code. I do believe Mr. Higginson would
agree. In the perusal of "Atlantic Monthly" I read an article by
a Mr. Higginson. The article was entitled, "Letter to a Young
Contributor." I was greatly drawn to his prose. He addressed his
readers as young gentlemen and young ladies and gave special
invitations to new or obscure contributors. He wrote that one
word can say more than half a life in a sentence or years of
crowded passion. My own lean words might be anticipated
to find favor. I knew his history as a minister at Free Church.
His abolitionist endeavors were much discussed by Father and
Austin. Each plumping for moral ideals and the sanctity of law.

In April of 1862, I made what I believe a bold decision. I did
hope for a new chapter under Mr. Higginson's tutelage after my
attempts to attract notice with local editors were of no success. In
the event, I learned a lesson in vicious worldliness. He agreed to
listen within the limit of current poetic custom but not to publish.

Importunate one that I am, my quest for astonishment
or at least agreement in even one pair of eyes fueled years of
energy and hope. I admit a quiver of disquiet. What if my
poems met general disapprobation? My pen set free questions
as much as well-being. My family would be held responsible for
my trackless lines of words.

I understood what each word represented, what image
lept from each line. I conveyed the futility of rage, my weary
frustrations, my bone-crushing loneliness, alongside a shield for
my joy and my eventual satisfaction with the ordinary. I pressed
moments of life to the page with words. Am I alone with their
import? Admittedly, I did not write placid lines in specific forms,
but my idea of a code comes from my presumption that the
words and images baffled others. Thus, as death beckons, in these
current jottings, I seek a simpler coherence in prose.

What glory to stop the code! To write plainly. To not
enslave the life of every word. The code cloaked my poems' terse

intentions. Today, amazement dances a jig as my old clipped lines
stretch into sentences. Complete sentences. Plainspokenness
eases the words into order. Swerving away will not serve.
Sentences wrap around like my favorite mantle, warming me for
a new and prosy path. Sentences are different from the stinging
fragments of poetry that strike from the page with a sharpness
that slaps. A poem may be a stormy blur of words—like a
parable—you have to find your own way in and out.

But sentences! Smooth honey holds words together. Flecked
with bits of wordy debris gleaned from an amber glow. Words
healed together in strings leave sweet knowings stuck to the comb
of my mind.

Prose kindles no reminders of the compulsions of poetry.
Or reminders of frustration over publication. I find myself glad
to have stayed alone with worries and doubts about my writing,
rather than have them paraded before unseeing eyes that might
accuse me of unsound conclusions.

My sentences curve like pendulum swings where I can
follow the arc between the extremes of affliction and felicity
where stability forms. Like cold honey, oozing by eighth inches,
sentences melt the unknown into the known. Sentences let my
poetic discoveries live longer and brighter than if they stayed
in the maidenly residence of my mind. My sentences can be as
round and full as age makes me.

I have a head full of language holding my breath captive.
While a universe of meaning moves in to shadow me. It's as if I
went through a door toward words and the door slammed behind
me. My brain and hands move with energy akin to escape from a
patch of scratchy nettles where I learned to accept the company
of creatures of root and light.

Apart from my excitement over sentences, I am dating my
epistles. Until now, titles or dates defined too tightly the impulse I
had been wresting onto the page.

I am still unwilling to title what I would have readers name
for themselves. Titles tidy or maybe remove the edges where
thought crooks a finger to lead a reader onto a private path.

The constraints of poetry—its compression—its demand of acute precision—are absent. My figurative confinements are dissolving. Notwithstanding memories, sickness, grief, and simply the press of time, my will strains for words that seldom fail. My spirit entertains a legacy of rapture.

January 22, 2006

Wife Wanted: pretty for purposes of compliance,
cookery, cleaning, and child-raising

LIKE EMILY'S MOTHER, MINE REPEATED THE CONVENTIONAL
wisdom of her day. This was to raise a lady-like daughter with
excellent homemaking skills. When I was ten, my mother gave me
some pages she had clipped and saved from a series in a women's
magazine. In her day magazines had large pages covered with text,
not an ad to be seen. Each clipping included an illustration of the
monthly topic. There was a cheerful woman in a frilly apron, a
couple holding hands, smiling children, and details unmistakably
of kitchen or dining room, like utensils, place settings, and
cleaning tools.

My mother pulled the pages from hibernation with the
hope that they would help guide me into and through young
womanhood. She was thinking about me and my future. Having
previously and with success beyond her wildest dreams paralyzed
my lively spirit, she believed that advice columns would polish
the remnants left of my readiness for marriage and family.

One page told me to read news about sports and cars so that
I could talk with boys and men to keep them in their comfort
zone. No mention of my comfort zone. One page was about
kissing and petting should I decide to do such things. The advice
admitted that such activities exist but disapproval deadened the

text. For young marrieds, there was a page of organizational tips to help me be ready for my man after his long day at work. No mention of my long day at home.

After I read the pages, I put them away. My untried instincts intuited that I would not find the help I needed by following the rules of etiquette.

My instincts were right. I returned to raising myself . . . a trial–and–error effort that was mostly error. Errors that reinforced my need to hang back and hide.

In first grade, my mother, who was President of the Home and School Association, sent me to school with a note about scheduling for the Principal. He came to the classroom, singled me out to ask for the note. A small, ordinary request, but I remember my shallow breathing and vacant brain as I retrieved the note from my coat pocket. Another time, she asked me to deliver a baby card to the new parents at the end of our block. Frisky drizzle smeared the ink on the envelope. My fear of delivering it in that state turned out to be greater than going home to a dressing-down about my general inadequacy and lack of confidence.

I recall my mother as socially accomplished. A lady, no doubt. She had a high-flutey, descant soprano voice that soloed at weddings, funerals, and choral events. The walls of our wartime house ballooned with brain-jarring bursts of Handel, old hymns or "Solveig's Song". If I was standing beside her when she sang, I could not hear anything else. I inched away from the assault of sound regardless of its purity.

She chaired school and church groups, tested the toast-making ability of Brownies earning badges, sang in a local women's choir, made wedding dresses for friends, was the first woman chalice bearer in our area, and was on a national committee that promoted the ordination of women. She cooked full-course meals, including a pretty table for twenty or more at holiday times. She convinced people to volunteer time and services. People sought her advice. She thrived in high-energy, people-oriented situations.

The downside was her homicidal Premenstrual Syndrome augmented by a touch of cabin fever. Common enough I'm sure in pre-media households where women were at home all day with young children in dark, cold climates. Her case was extreme. Sadly, PMS was not a recognized condition in the fifties. When her PMS and my toddlerness coincided, the result for me was the visitation of beatings, smotherings, and half-drownings delivered by my dad's belt, my pillow, and the kitchen tap of an old laundry-sized sink.

These frequent but random incursions engulfed me in an other-worldly swirl of neutrality where I waited until it was safe to come back. I would fall, spread-eagle, into a spiral of flat-black-velvet-dissociative darkness. My spirit, or part of it, was gone from my body for a while. I lost all sense of time, unaware of what was around me. Then I would wake up in my bed as if I had been merely napping under a scratchy old blanket that further irritated my welts. My mother did not nurture me so much as provide food, shelter, and the unchallenged behavioral expectations of her generation.

My child's brain could not reconcile the fact that the person supposed to be most concerned with my welfare, regularly tried to kill me. How bad could I be? Unspeakably bad, it seemed. I have no memory of early life that does not involve fearful waiting for the next humiliation or possibly death. It felt very close. I lived in an orbit apart from my surroundings.

Eventually, I learned to read. Books informed and amused me. They were an escape even if I could not concentrate or remember much of what was on the pages.

I grew up to be a classic example of the discontinuity that can exist between public and private personas. My mother wanted me to reflect on her accomplishment in raising a compliant, cooperative daughter whose life differed little from her own. I could not be that young woman, though publicly I looked the part with trendy clothes and actions copied as best I could from popular culture.

One motherly attempt to 'communicate' during the groovy sixties happened when I was in high school. Hugging was the latest. She tried. I was rigid. She did not try again. It was too late. There were no words yet—no way—to explain the friendless, academic half-life of my private persona. I was an intellectual nerd, a wallflower—without peer. Literally.

As Emily's father supported education for women, so did my mother. She showed some foresight so that I would have something to fall back on if tradition failed. The effects of flower children, feminism, and the pill could not have been foreseen as factors that furthered the separations in our lives.

a hurt child
hurries along
to fight
recurring urges

to hurt self
in fist flailing rage
to flay
useless flesh

no one home
under her hide
no home for one soul
who'd sell it for normal

August 4, 1884

As I REST, BRIGHT PAIN FROLICS OVER MY BROW. PRONE IS THE best posture to tether its exuberance. Its uninvited existence rules the hours of its residence. Eventually, it will sneak off with its friends, Melancholy and Bilious. Sadly, while Pain and Bilious may take their leave, too often Melancholy is left behind. As if I need an anchor for my darkness, after so many deaths and now illness. It is clear that pain and sadness are my companions as I draw near to my long home. I wonder how to befriend them— instead of beating against them like bars that cage me—as I befriended solitude during its gradual establishment.

In times of illness, life gathers around. It becomes a bristly blanket, not milled to softness. It lays over me until I attend. My mind folds it into episodes that can be laid away in tidy squares. The litany of episodes is lengthy. Losses mostly, that began with the death of my tutor, Ben, a stripling of thirty-two. The company of girlhood companions was lost to the establishment of their homes and marriages. I lost hope of treading that path. To the wraiths of illness, albeit transitory until now, I have lost my health. And many of my loves are lost to death.

I could not have predicted where the force of circumstance would lead. Possibility beckoned in early days as it is wont to do for young people. I never considered the presence of friends limited to paper. I did not consider an invading turmoil of spirit. One that wages battle in my heart and dims my mind with confusion until my poems attempted to calm turmoil's advance with clarity of words. Clarity for me at least. Catching ideas with the consolation of words is akin to trapping insects with a net of enormous mesh.

Far away in my brain, I remember urgency. A longing that made my frame ache as with a boundless quest. I loosed my linguistic reins, let thought have its head to flirt with coherence but conclusion eluded. No matter how loosely I held and waited,

I could not alter the world's direction. I could not compete amid the discordance of men charged with control. I could not be heard amid the lock-step ranks of women. It seemed necessary instead to hold my small household on course. I turned to my lurching meter—my observations bound orderly in bundles to find fortification for enduring. Gratitude for insight lived in my visits to my literary fort armed with my friendly lexicon. Such retreat relieved heart's tumult. Reinforcement in the form of my own company. I read my poems to remember what I know. And I read Browning's *Aurora Leigh* and Thoreau, and Charles Dickens, and George Eliot. I had their knowledge. Father required reading of the Bible. Psalms taught me to number my days that I might apply my heart to wisdom.

Early ambition pinned me as a poet whose publication would bring honor, and not a little surprise, to my family name. My poems would be opened like gifts eliciting gasps at the shine of gems. Poems would be held up to the light. Word facets refracting meaning in all directions. A small heart corner would preen and press for the gifts to be opened again and again to vocal agreement and to quiet amendment of the lives around me. Isolation may not have ensued had I more trust in my work compared with what I viewed as the commonplace writing of others. Their tired floral posies ruffled no feathers—while the gems I flashed to stir conscience were left uncut—the ore of my soul left as dross.

Evening sneaks in as I write, the sun, a beacon weary of lighting my way slowly pulls up a counterpane. Our shared light fades into memory of day. I am consoled to know that this sun will slip like breath back into tomorrow.

While I am still in moderately sweet robustness, I do consider the day when my light will fade and leave dimming remembrance in the minds of those who know me. Of late I find a curious calm amid minutes marching by—a deftness in the manner of the day's unfolding—a lingering with gentleness over my dough or my needle or the bloomiest buds. Urgency has receded. Each moment seems to finish at the precise moment the next begins. Not surprising but nonetheless I forget that time has separate moments or hours that flow heedless of my enfeebled attempts to marshall them into tidy blocks of achievement.

Like all created things, my remains will return to dust and be refashioned into the life of the universe. But the spirit that enlivens me, cries not to be lost in moist decay. Words that crowded my days could be buried with me. Behind me—dips eternity—before me—immortality—myself the term between. I wish to take my term, human and transcendent and write it into an enduring form. I will pour prose into moments as they hop past in the space of each breath—the only space where the Divine can catch me.

By this I mean to cheat mortality in some small respect. I crave affiliation with George Eliot's choir invisible, whose music is the gladness of the world. She and other choir members have been a cup of strength to me. And so I wish to be to others.

February 12, 2006

I HAVE BEEN CARRIED, CALMED, CHALLENGED, AND CONSOLED BY the words of others. Emily is prominent among them. I turn to my adopted section of the choir invisible when my equilibrium has suffered a blow. When this happens balance disintegrates. Balance is one of my favorite words. I wonder what Emily would have thought about balance. As a subject, the word balance does not occur in her poems. Her poetry shows more of an acquaintance with extremes and a fusion of secular and sacred images. "We grow accustomed to the Dark . . . When Light is put away." "It might be lonelier . . . It might be easier." "'Tis not that dying hurts us so . . . Tis living hurts us more." Extremes are appealing. Their dramatic intensity is suited to the pith exposed in poetry as opposed to the sprawl of prose that may lessen the impact of images.

Emily wrote about hope as a thing with feathers. She looked for certain slants of light. Birds, bees, friends, death, places, soul, flowers, names, and love densely infuse her work. She stood with hands and heart open toward a day without need to control the word images that balanced her creative process and the end result. She balanced this open posture with remarkable solitude. I think moderns find it difficult, if not repellent, to identify with the degree of frustrated alienation in her life, though it was fertile territory for her. Solitude, tempered by her practice of writing, gently plundered her unconscious for buoyant rafts of words.

I believe balance moderates. It moves reflection toward manageable pockets near the center of life's continuum. The rocking undulations of the middle are more livable than the jagged crags of outlying edges. Opposing forces meet in the middle to integrate. A lifetime of steady undulations is stirred by brief punches from visits to the edge. I wonder if the intention of prose is to meander through moderation and information while poems if they are accessible, are straight-line winds to emotion?

When I am wandering in mental darkness, balance re-establishes itself as a 'knowing.' A 'knowing' is knowledge, unmistakable knowledge, that arrives in my brain as a thought or words that suggest direction or reinforce understanding. These reminders can seem small and external. A friend calls with an invitation, or a favorite brand of shoes is found in my size and on the third markdown, or I follow a detour and find a particularly leafy new route to work, or I have all the ingredients on hand for a batch of cookies, or a parking spot opens near the door on a cold day. Reminders can also be an internal tweak like when a quick click to the E-edition of the newspaper which reliably lands in my email at 5:02a, shows it to be absent. So I can not distract myself with the crossword as revisions elbow their way to the top of my priorities. Work first. And I need such prods.

The practicality of a knowing provokes a spontaneous 'ah . . . now I feel it!' Something has moved from my head to my heart. If I do not pay attention, the knowing will return with the insistence of a brick thrown in my direction. When I feel muddled, out of sorts, or confused, it is a sure sign that a 'knowing' is imminent. Transformation—acceptance is pushing its way to the edge of my consciousness.

I spent the last year trying not to write. Insomnia and indigestion morphed into daily pain and exhaustion that screamed for attention. I came upon a memoir that described one woman's life as a series of plateaus mingled with the trust and leaps that led her along from one plateau to the next. Taking her cue for myself, I resumed journaling and played with an idea for an expanded memoir, written in form, describing how to identify plateaus and

how to move among them. Indeed, a semblance of balance formed
between the arcs of pain and denial that had been flinging me
back and forth.

Cultural imbalance is not so easily addressed. During
my lifetime, the utility of churches, schools, and government
has been changing. Congregations split over whether biblical
exhortations are meant to be static or adaptive. Schools engage
in "one size fits all" models that are not supported by data on
individual differences or child development. Government?
Well, this country's flight from over-centralized and top-down
tyrannies has managed to recreate them complete with attendant
greed and corruption. It took only a couple of hundred years.

Social climate bows before status and materialism. Leaders
resist the re-arrangement of dominant social, educational, or
employment models. We, the *vox populi*, are ineffectual because
we are taught to be herded not self-directed. We expect to be
treated like a group not as individuals. How could an individual
gain voice against power brokers who have lost contact with
the common good? How can I refuse to be led around by the
economic ring in my nose? Where is balance?

There are thinkers who hover over herded masses. Masses
who are mainly extroverts may I add. Their bumptious obsession
with consumption and scarcity leaves the heavy lifting of social
democracy to the modest, largely ignored, and introverted artists,
and writers. Emily stood out from her puritanical herd.

That the core-questioning intensity of her poetry was not
embraced should surprise no one. That we continue to refuse
core questions is also no surprise. Popular culture entangles us in
short-term ties to fashion, talking toys, media delivery systems,
and vehicles and houses sized out of all proportion to our need.
We colluded with the 1980s greed and mobility that within a
generation all but destroyed ideas of self-sacrifice, the common
good, basic thrift, and vision.

Vision—what a quaint notion—it used to be an assumed
part of our civilization. Vision considers lessons learned alongside
current reality and suggests a future where prospects are fair and

there is hope. Then it suggests how to get there from here. Vision balances wisdom and the unknown. Those who thrive in this balance have an inclusive worldview—their home base is grounded in curiosity, flexibility, and deep respect for differences.

Balance is held in our self-stories when we include the socially acceptable middles along with forays into our best and worst. Everyone has a story worth telling, and every time it's told ego strength grows. And let someone listen—listening without judgment may be a new frontier. We would do well to write our stories or tell them. Literally get the words out of our bodies so space can be filled with new words, new tellings.

> pedantry is a promise
> broken
> where edges scratch
> the shine of clarity

August 10, 1884

MY SENTENCES TAKE ME BACK TO BIRTH. AS IF THE SEED planted to grow into me produced an unexpected bloom. The Emily seed that was supposed to fruit into marriage and children instead sprouted into word stories spreading on paper leaves.

As a child, I believed that I was born old. Not in the sense of a gnome-like creature, gnarled and grey, but a being whose sturdy limbs, ruddy hair, and rosy cheeks gave every appearance of being just a child. I took the measure of my situation serenely or with agitation as if from a distant point of vantage. A point beyond sight and hearing. My locality of home and land were central, but not as vital as the qualities of the tenants keeping the homes and lands. To see that, my eyes sieved starlight for souls suitable for association.

Knowledge of the Other comes through children like me. We are scattered across earth quietly spreading wisdom. It takes years for the outside of our frame to get as old as the knowing on the inside. Wise ones are sought—even as children—like rocks above a flood.

As such a child, I rambled around inside the realms of sight and sound, in lovely moments of well-being, unjostled by common care. In my glad play, wisdom was there whether or not I wanted it. Hopping from rock to rock down streams of memory as far back as I can, I found that words opened me to the world.

Words were my fruit. Self-revelation for me and assurance for others. There were times when words lifted me from the world and left me with a gasping sense of wonder that gathered like light at the corners of my eyes. Then gradually, I returned to the world, set down in an ordinary task, ragdoll relaxed and sated with elation. Lucky the child whose spiritedness is encouraged—lucky even to be ignored—not lucky the one whose parents quell the spirit in ruptured seeds of early behavior.

Long sight and illumination are contraries in a work-a-day world. My companions did not care for news I brought from foreign realms of thought. The sense that I visited where they had not was intriguing but not inspiring. I believed then, and so continue to believe that mysterious realms of knowing are nearby, waiting with buds of knowledge, waiting patiently to sprout into wisdom. When I was away at school, I realized that forerunners—those who select support for the unseen—who strew the air with the experience of light—may be uncomfortable friends.

August 4, 2007

EMILY'S IMAGE OF THE CLOSET AS THE PATENT REMEDY OF HER
day for suppressing spiritedness in girls is not the worst
technique available. Whipping a small body into welts, then
smothering or half-drowning cries of panic and pain are
guaranteed options for suppressing spirit—maybe even life. In
my case—not life—not literally.

> silence
>   plain girl
> silence
>   reading girl
> silence
>   thinking girl
> silence
>   take a tiny trowel—silver
>   chilly silver
>   to shovel thought
>   like a small indecency
>   under carpet corners
>   lest it threaten convention

The problem as I internalized it was the fact that I existed.
But should not. The consequences of deficit parenting warped my
girl child's experience to the point where I believed I was a freak
who deserved to be off the mainstream path, if not actually dead.
I survived by never letting anyone get close enough to see the
excrescence behind my presentable public persona. My mask. But
my brain could not concentrate. It was distracted by unrelenting

surveillance. I was taking in signals around me. Body language. Tones of voice. I was ready to disappear at a moment's notice. Dissociative disappearance if not physical. My small voice was strangled into silence by my need to stay invisible. To draw no attention to myself whatsoever.

I remember myself as a honey-blonde girl in puffy-sleeved dresses with matching socks who went forth, and then back, to kick over rocks of warped development in an effort, however futile, to be culturally mainstream. I tried to find the moisture-loving maggots under those rocks. Maggots quietly making a meal of my slow death. I wanted them to take my filthy deformed carbon atoms and recycle them into a useful human.

A small, cornered human who screamed "Daddy, Daddy!" The reply returning as if from a distance yelled, "He can't hear you. He's downtown. No one can hear you. There's no help for you—I'll hit you with the buckle end and scar your face so that no man will ever look at you—if you cry, I'll call the orphanage to come and get you." Through my mother's breath-taking episodes of belt-yielding welts and credible efforts at suffocation, my spirit was sacrificed. A shard of consciousness slipped away—somewhere—for years—I floundered in its absence unable to trust or love or be present.

My father collaborated by not noticing or coming to my defense. His young male life had been drained by survival efforts extracted during the Great Depression as a field worker and laborer who used a pick-ax to hack out a store basement from the well-frozen ground. This was followed by five years of combat in the European Theater of World War II. There his own psyche was a stage for the daily duel between horrific Axis leaders and principled Allied leaders over their respectively submissive people.

> in eternity blue
> sky a backdrop
> for the dizzy grace
> of deft planes strafing
> for advantage

below on stylish French meadows
airman dine
al fresco on oranges

Perhaps after years of war, years of orders, and fragmenting societies, he lost his voice and chose to believe that my mother was applying a correct strategy to produce a dutiful daughter. From my child's perspective, his reserve and unavailability registered as confirmation of my flawed existence. I was not worth his notice, much less his protection.

Emily's spirit was stifled as well, via the closet and rigid social rules and the "this" from her comment to me, that she did not want to happen to anyone else. Each of us spent a considerable portion of our lives combing through our circumferences as if we could will the appointed time, the *kairos* of consciousness that kept its own unknown schedule. We tried to explain with words, joining a long line of wordsmiths who struggled to capture experience and the ephemera of feeling with the limitations of language.

Emily dropped out of expected norms after years of hope that those in her circumference would listen and let her participate in the philosophical and social concerns bandied about at home, school, and church. Eventually, she wrote and resorted to the comfort of her gardens, in her generous correspondence, in her family, and in Carlo, her faithful, friendly dog.

For my part, as the resident irredeemable in my circumference, I could not wait to fulfill expected norms. Having been whipped out of usual development, I watched 'normal life' from a distance as Emily did. In memory, I remember a timid dysphoria settled resolutely under fashionable clothes on a pleasantly proportioned body while I waited, waited, and waited for a clue about what was wrong with me. During many years of waiting, a few people reacted to my oddness.

A family friend reacted. A lovely man, whose voice had a rumbly resonance befitting a bishop. He bought a doll for me. A fashion doll. Store-bought clothes for the doll came on his subsequent visits. He had a much-wanted daughter of his own which led me to wonder why he bought toys for me. I believed that this man might take away the pretty toys if he learned how bad I was, although, I also wonder if he noticed my jumpiness, the wary look in my eyes, and tried to help by simply paying special attention.

During my early school years, my Brownie leader noticed. She told my mother that she could not tell off anyone if I was in the room because it upset me. Years later I learned that this reaction is normal for trauma victims with their skewed perception of threat.

As I waited through high school, kids noticed and left unkind limericks in my coat pockets. "To my darling . . . to my love" and closing with the fact that they would feel small if I found out who wrote them. I recall showing up at school once with an exceptionally trendy outfit. Aqua shoes that were a ballerina flat, Mary Jane combo, with an orange knit, A-line dress with white Chanel style facings. A popular girl, who must have drawn the short straw, approached me and asked where I got the clothes. Instant paralysis resulted in a stiff, blurted city name. I had traveled there by train with my mother for a family event. We'd had time for shopping. I knew I had scored, particularly with those shoes. But only enjoyed them in the confines of exclusion.

At university, I waited. My boyfriend noticed. He called me passive, said that I never made suggestions for going out. I stopped returning his calls before he got closer or made any more observations.

I did try talking to a campus chaplain. He said he had the impression that if someone slapped my face, I would stand there and turn the other cheek. I believe he referred to the numbness he observed. He was worse than no help because he reinforced my sense of being odd and hopeless.

As I waited through a year away from university, there was a day in the dull, grayness of late winter when I lost hope for a place in the world. Years of waiting for a difference, for some kind of breakthrough, for explanation, coalesced into a deep shameful recognition of a futile and fruitless existence. An episode of aspirin poisoning passed off as feeling 'flu-ish' for a forsaken couple of days, fixed me at a point of half-life for several more years. My body functioned with no animation of spirit and little connection to the present. The personification of an outsider.

Upon my return to university, a superintendent monitoring my student teaching noticed. His few visits found me sitting in a back corner. Probably looking blank. I acted my way through the lesson he was required to observe. After talking with the classroom teacher, he said that he would not have passed me if he had not seen me in front of the class. One time. I managed to pull off a lesson on farms.

I waited, ever hopeful that something in the next plateau would pierce my oddball status; under the hope was a gut-punching fear that someone would notice me. That thought was as scary as not being noticed. I decided naively, that marriage might help. To someone who would never notice my mask, much less look behind it. That is precisely what I did. It was not a conscious decision but a bow to tradition. A hope that marriage might help me connect. If that did not work, then at least a husband and children would be worthy props to hide behind. I did not know that a man who would not notice or challenge my mask would be a man more damaged than I. A man whose mask was firmly in place too.

The campus chaplain's comment proved prophetic. Once married, I did stand there and turn the other cheek until I learned to duck and stay distant. Then the only hurt was words. I was not blameless. My many years with many moments of near-paralysis and missing pieces of experience conditioned my reflexive response of withdrawal. Healthy emotional development stayed blocked.

The first crack in my exile from humanity was delivered along with my first daughter. Motherhood made my life acceptably secondary. A second daughter came along and for the next twenty years my energy, time, and money were spent for their benefit. As is the case for some mothers, I became a functionary. Unnoticed and unapproachable while I skillfully deflected attention to my smart and beautiful girls. The many obligations and occupations of parenting handily repressed my sense of waiting. This did not mean that I perceived myself to be a separate valuable person—but I didn't need to—all effort went to ensure that my girls did not turn into me. Oddly, or maybe not oddly, they each 'finished' a piece of my unlived life through family and career.

Emily seemed to know that a marriage of convenience would not work. Although she did not marry, her early life seems to have been healthier. She did not appear to have developmental gaps. The first half of her life was lively, full of enthusiasm for her social circumference and a quiet hope being a poet. And I think anticipation that a convivial, conjugal relationship would be vouchsafed. The worst that was said about her was that she too demanding of time and approval from the older, married men she turned to for conversation. During the second half of life, she retreated, became more isolated. Her connection to others came through newspapers, books, letters, and family. Writing eased the restlessness and preoccupations that often accompany too much time spent alone.

I decided that I wanted liveliness to be the hallmark of the second half of my life. My entrenched invisibility with its knobs of fear and self-disgust had to be altered. Being a parent was the beginning of a change in my sense of identity. I found that I could not entirely suppress nudges toward self-examination and consequent self-acceptance that hovered patiently on the fringes. Books were an access point. In the beginning of my awakening, Thomas Merton's *New Seeds of Contemplation*, Marion Woodman's *Addiction to Perfection,* and Alice Miller's books were important. I remember the release I felt from my sense of core badness when I read that a lack of concentration and an inability to finish things are distinctive features of child abuse.

A small, unbidden healing event came one day from my corner of the collective unconscious. I stepped into the walk-in closet I used. The closet had one arrow-slit window. Its narrowness made an effort at light but the tired grayness that wormed its way in from the north was hardly defeated by the beam of one naked light bulb. My spirit, cautioned by the dusty light, reeled into the dark past.

I had walked into that closet many times. That day the dimness spiraled me into the similar dull opacity trapped by the ragged green roller-shades in the bedroom of my childhood. My spirit split. One half stayed in the closet, the other half returned to the childhood room. My old room was a place where light snuck around the edges, as if it knew what a safe room felt like and mine was not it. I felt the ominous dread of punishment about to descend.

In the closet, my hands groped for the edge of the dresser as I began to fall. I thought I was fainting from the wave of dissociation that engulfed from the old room. I did not topple tree-like to the floor but let my hands ease along the dresser's edge as I slipped to my knees, then to a full fetal curl on cold, worn hardwood. Rationality stranded me in the ensuing minutes. I was left in sobbing, gagging, body-rigid grief—for my life in both rooms at once.

In the old room, my mother's flailing arm was extended by three feet of writhing leather. The image stayed just beyond focus as paroxysms of panic choked the closet with the question, "How could you? How could you? How could you?"

When the balance of my mind came back, I felt a 'knowing.' For the first time, I understood that my history was not my fault, had never been my fault. This moment of oceanic relief arrived in tandem with the tougher part of the knowing. Though not my fault, I was responsible, nonetheless, for mending the damage. Every day.

My damaged life could not be mended from within my marriage. I had a suspicion that we each had to find a way to repair ourselves as individuals before there could be any hope for relationship. Nearly thirty years ago I left with two young girls. A marriage of dueling dysfunction had become insupportable. Hiding behind husband and children could not work.

I had no job, no friends. I did not talk much. Could not think on my feet. During outings I waited to go home, making sure I knew how to exit. This had to change. A remarkable and tenacious counselor walked with me through my initial transformation.

In the eighties when I left my marriage, Post Traumatic Stress Disorder had been a legitimate diagnosis for a mere four years. The disorder dates from 1896 when Sigmund Freud published "Etiology of Hysteria." His peers would not accept that trauma produced the symptoms of hysteria he described in his twelve case studies of young women. He retracted the article but his work was the basis for the shell shock of World War I which became battle fatigue in World War II, combat neurosis in the Vietnam era after which PTSD was the settled upon diagnosis. It is now an umbrella term for trauma-based conditions. Trauma caused by combat, abuse, accidents, or natural disasters. PTSD named my history of abuse. From that point, I began a multi-year pilgrimage of re-invention.

I stumbled ahead amazed to find that what I needed fell onto my path. Books and people. A job came, good daycare, and a newly rehabbed apartment filled with sunlight. I kept reading and talking to people who helped with acceptance and reconciliation. Light did in fact emerge from darkness. I came to terms with the time it took to fill in developmental gaps, to work with the hyper-vigilance that kept me isolated and invisible, to develop an emotional age and a chronological age that were roughly synchronous.

I felt like I was living the old joke about the girl who finds a piece of rope in a room full of horse manure and exclaims that there must be a pony in there somewhere. I retraced a path to the original bedroom and to the closet breakpoint from which I painstakingly and constantly worked at affirmations. I mourned for the years of life never mine to lose—the lost little girl, the wallflower teen, the background mother. A chameleon's life—expert in camouflage. That period of my life was similar to coming out of a deep meditation.

When I opened my eyes, colors were brighter, edges crisper, there seemed to be more light around me. It was like driving down a familiar street and realizing that the house with purple shutters or the power substation have always been there. Details started to register. I am stuck in cliched statements about veils lifting, doors opening that fail to hint at the ravishing emergence of consciousness from whatever brain convolutions had held it in trust.

behind me
a landscape
pitted by wells

filled with dying
rot and mold
that refused release
from round sunken rooms

my body's abraded
the grip of mind
and appendages slip
on ledges and cracks
that scrape in the dark

I only know up
by gray light
easing to white
by scented air
soothing my chest
with a promise of rest

from each out-crawling
I yelled
victory
from the mouth of a well

August 12, 1884

BEFORE I AROSE, I LAY DROWSILY WATCHING LACE CURTAINS make patterns of light. The patterns seem less like lace and more like chain links—dragging across the floor. Heart-lifting sunlight pierces through links as the lace tries to impede their blatancy. Light slips between the links in a valiant effort to unchain me from my shadows.

Today I have the energy to roam in my room—to work at my little desk. The room where light and heat are leeched from dozens of sunny summers stored in kindling and logs. The room where thousands of words have flown from my pen.

A room saturated by missives for myself and others. A room sanctified by heart's love laid down on many an inner battlefield. I have spent sweet hours here within these sheltering walls. Hope and desecration dueled within it precincts, now shadows foreshadow a tomb.

Declaring a prosy intention is one thing—filling up the lines is quite another. My inevitable but not imminent demise urges me on. Writing one's history is a fearful but fascinating spur. Words unwritten become insistent. If not penned, they will push themselves to the brink of my thoughts and fall out into dreams or the dishpan or onto the floor to be swept away with the rest of the daily dust.

I wonder if plain telling will be sensible to others or if my devotion to the inner holy and solitude is merely self-indulgent. Do I offer a hearty, thick stew of words to a starving populace?

Or do I offer cookies to feed an inner gnawing—sustenance only for the one writing? Am I casting hard-won words at ears open only to the commonplace? In spite of sundry small worries, I am determined to reflect, to wind through the eras, take the lanes of my temporality, and let the spinner spin a tale through me of interior life.

My tale may be compared and found inconsistent or worse, incomprehensible. I hope more that it gives a glimpse of creeping consciousness normally obscured by fences erected to contain the mind's private property. Each bit of quickening needs to soar beyond the familiar of its own backyard.

Conversation, friendship, and books need to be tossed back and forth over the fence to enlarge capacity of mind. One must fill the yard or demolish the fence to find new ideas, new points of reference. My 'knowings' are the points of my own experience. My circumference. My consciousness. By writing these pages, I am connecting the points of my experience to form a bed that will receive me fearless when the spinner collects me captured and calls me back to the center.

August 16, 2007

MY REFLECTIONS ARE PIXELATED BEFORE CONGRUITY HITS paper. This began in a typing class taught by a bleached and beehived woman whose fingers had another life rolling, teasing, pinning, and spraying hair according to the twisted styles of the 1960s. She never did my hair but I remember her typing class. It was mostly female as teenage boys would become men who counted on having one of us to type for them. It being unlikely that we would have work of our own to type.

Typing fell into the fall-back skills category. Like a university education, nice to have but not likely to be needed since my professional husband would take care of me. My typing skill was adequate. Not close to the virtuosity of girls who clicked along at 120 words per minute with no errors. I did not expect to be that proficient. Not with hyper-vigilance inhibiting my focus. Part of my mind was always scanning for a potential threat. Most of my mind sometimes.

A modern semantic change turned typing into keyboarding. The same action for letter-producing taps. The perception of typing has changed as well. It once was the preserve of women who unfortunately had to provide for themselves. Think of mind-numbing, clone-like rows of women who never moved beyond the typing pool. Who never dreamed they could. Now a keyboard is the access point to any number of electronic gadgets in constant proximity if not constant use by both genders.

At my high school, we learned to type on boxy manual typewriters on desks that were too tall. At least for me. I had to sit up very straight. Inert brown machines hunkered on tabletops lying in wait for our novice fingering. A town of offices waited to pay us for typing and other paper functions like filing. It took a fair amount of pressure to work the keys. Uneven pacing would lock a bunch of them together. Mistakes were obvious. Carbon copies showed them all. Once in a great while, my reptilian brain still searches for the carriage return.

I worked in offices for nearly ten years before the latest innovation, electric typewriters, replaced manuals. Typing was faster, and eraser tape made errors less obvious. Chips and microprocessors currently reign supreme. Long strings of characters race across the page if a tad too much pressure is applied to a key. Just as quickly, deleting disappears them. Proofreading is more important than keystrokes. Mistakes look like ignorance rather than ineptness.

Before typing, penmanship taught students how to get words on paper. My third-grade cartridge pen was magical proof that I was ready to tackle cursive handwriting. Hours of loops between the lines followed. Pens were to be held correctly.

My teacher watched each hand. She patrolled the aisles and forced index fingers into correct arcs. Over and over until our fingers automatically assumed the position. The better to produce legible text. An ink-ingrained writer's bump formed on the middle finger of the dominant hand. Pens in hand, we covered pages with practice letters. The best examples were tacked to the bulletin board. Only superior work was displayed. The also-rans knew exactly who they were but no one worried about creating complexes by honoring excellence.

When I sit in groups, I watch people write. A vast array of writing utensils are held in an equally vast array of grips. Some hands resemble claws dragging across paper. Others try to have every finger in contact with the pen, mimicking the crabbed and curled digits of the arthritic. The white knuckles of others emboss the words onto the following page.

I find an easy-grip is best for mindless fingering, then
the brain focuses on content. Still, my papers are covered with
marginal balloons, tiny interlineations, and smeary scratch-outs.
Pages resemble a formidable maze. Revision is likely to produce
a whole new maze. Follow the arrows, the subscript symbols, the
numbered sentences toward attempted articulation. Once in a
while, the words satisfy from first writing.

I read them from a vantage point of weeks or months or years
and celebrate the little mental explosion somewhere in the universe
that brought them to mind and onto paper. Done. For now.

August 28, 1884

PAPER OF ALL SORTS FOUND ITS WAY INTO MY POSSESSION AND waited patiently for inscription. Images can be fleeting if not recorded upon arrival. Effort to conjure them later is generally unsatisfactory. It is akin to catching butterflies—something colorful but insubstantial flutters into view—followed by frantic batting and chasing. The result may be dead reality pinned to paper. But if a catcher is careful, observers and readers will feel pleasantly informed, while unaware of the fact that their information arose from much exertion to adhere it to the page.

I like the physical process of writing. The knobbly paper held firmly under my left hand. The pen drags and chafes its way through each line like a sixth finger that leaves meaning marks in glossy black liquid. Liquid distilled from ash, our own source, and ending. Odd that our ashy means of making words visible has the same ashy origination that makes us visible.

What do people do who do not write? I believe we are all subject to incursions of thought, to momentary visitation by ideas which perhaps do not need to be recorded to accomplish their task. To leave an impression. Like dreams. Those gifts of sleep which may frighten or confuse. I was both frightened and confused by the lank pink worm I tied to a piece of furniture in a dream. Perhaps being averse to control, the worm became a mottled snake that read my fear as I fled from threat unto a distant town. My breath raced in the darkness when I awoke. The dream images last without enlightening.

Without telling or writing, does wisdom distilled from experience enter the world? I think not. I propose that only those who write or talk about their sensations move to new ones. Many among us who claim authority stay in one spot, existing thusly for years. Never becoming a more thoughtful person as a consequence of reflection. Never risking sensation implicit in words.

Salvation is counted true if it fits into the proscribed mold given by the authority of church or other governance as well as by the recitation of beliefs and adherence to creeds deemed correct. Such authority is confounded by the concept of varied revelation. The idea that other expression and interpretation may lead to the same end. Salvation and loyalty to one's group, limited to the language of one's group, is all. This box has no entrance for me. In the absence of the potentially renewing forces of marriage and progeny, I have explored change in my mental landscape, within the confines and content of my circumference.

September 1, 1884

A NEW MONTH BRINGS SCHOOL AND HARVEST. LEAVES FOLLOW autumn rules and prepare for their new life as dust. My mother followed women's rules and prepared for domestic function. As if a wife and mother script dropped whole into her being. She was to follow it and build a span bridging to a new generation. Her span's supporting columns of duty and standards were twin to the ones built by my grandmother and to the ones she expected to be of my construction.

Submission to husband and suppression of individuality mark a successful crossing of the narrow span above tantalizing depth. The crossing is bounded on both ends by excellent home management and marriage to a polished townie. I have wondered if men marry only to feel disappointed with broodmares who tidy and cook, but offer little or no engagement with the faculty of mind? Few I should think. Enough intellectual stimulation presumed to come by way of cigars in parlors of an evening.

I suppose as well that even the hunger for conjugal activity wanes into obligation. Sister-in-law, Susan, would agree as would Austin. Spousal responsibilities divided by gender are presumed to be sufficient structure to carry pairs through their separate daily rounds. Soul friends are not a first qualifier for relationship. If such deep attraction is chanced upon, it must be savored amid a mild blaze of public attention, though for some, like Austin, it overtook vows and gave access to the arena of the illicit.

Our mother modeled an ideal of individual suppression. Conservatively gowned, she cooked, served, and managed pleasant occasions. But I have an impression of distraction hovering relentlessly over the many details of hosting. A welcome of food and order, but not chat. No wonder Father ranted over Mother's escape to kitchen, to children, to bed. He wanted her to shoulder a larger portion of the socializing expected by the men of the college and their wives. Had she done so, he may not have sought a sacrificial lamb.

When I sensed my mother's qualities stirring in me, I let my brain examine them as if I were choosing chops for dinner. I rejected Mother's selection. It was tough and gristly. Unpalatable. I searched among the plump and fresh. I let my mind roam to what was hidden at the back holding rich color and juiciness.

My desire was to wander among my choices. However few. Among my age-mates, no choice was perceived. From early days I poked, tested, and sampled all the notions of the female exampled by my surround of mothers and friends. I never desired their goodness unless it was part truth as well. Truth as I understood it. I see details—colors, shapes, and objects of all sorts in the arrangement of life in my family. Interior details as well. Snatches of content, frustration, gratitude, and greed. A parade of inner and outer qualities that I thought others saw as vividly. When I pronounced on such topics as a young woman, a curtain was drawn. I became invisible. Clearly, women should not possess opinions or ask questions. I looked like my peers but the foundation of a wall separating us began early and assembled itself slowly.

Books were better friends than family. I read my favorites— *Aurora Leigh*, *The Mill on the Floss*, and Hawthorne's *The Scarlet Letter*, and Longfellow's *Kavanagh*. More seriously, *Of the Imitation of Christ* by Thomas á Kempis. Some like Kavanagh were read in surreptitious doses. Installments stored in the piano bench. They let me look at lives, albeit fictional, beyond Amherst. Books were peopled with characters who lived in villages, had gardens, found sentimental attachments, were subject to literary or social failure, followed by acceptable redemption.

Thomas á Kempis was in a separate league. If novels were a diversionary romp in grassy meadows, Thomas was a stint of mountain climbing. I climbed without hesitation and at the summit aligned myself with his notion of a daily regimen—with the idea of my room as cloister. It was calming and from it, I did indeed find Being's Center. I sought my own society. Writing formed the foundation that began the wall of solitude.

Even desultory conversation was difficult. I read discomfort in the eyes of callers. Cookery, fashion, or sundry other chores weighed more heavily on their minds than mine. Callers in mid-conversation would pause, "Oh, Henry or George or William or John can not possibly make his own tea!" They summarily excused themselves and toddled off home suffused with a glow of usefulness. Their path of being needed was an ever-deepening rut, in my opinion at least. Eventually, they will not be remarked upon other than to complement their degree of success in putting forth a husband and offspring worthy of note.

The glow of marrieds always eclipsed my unmarried state. If they were to glimpse into my life, they would find much to recommend about what I do to keep my family order. It would be unseemly to draw attention to the lightness of my bread or the strength of the seams I sew or the hearty produce from my gardens. Or the year-round floral tributes from my little garden off the dining room whose dried remains petal the jottings of my preferred communication.

As I remembered my friends' highest aspirations—to be a maid in essence—nausea rippled in my midriff. No time then for reading or my posies, only pride in children's progress and the desirability of my social occasions.

I shrank from such. I know my wish to discuss the affairs of state, of the church, would be politely diverted at best. At worst, I would be told not to meddle with objects of men's minds that might unsettle mine. Where is a place for me? I do not want the kitchen—and the study is closed.

September 7, 1884

A FAMILY ON A FORCED MARCH TO CHURCH. FIVE STANDARD-bearers stepping along. Two sets of tight collars together with three bonnets, torsos concealed by coats, cloaks, and skirts skimming the dusty road. Three females and two males march duty-bound down the street to our hard-backed benches. Our faces formed into flat composure. Eyes front and only slightly unfocused on the minister's facial contortions as his exhortation drones in our ears.

I cast about for any diversion. Are there new hats or gowns flashing extravagance? Or at least some that are decently dull and thus echo-worthy? Are the children sufficiently cowed for public view? Any sidelong glances between smitten youth? When I have exhausted sights within eyeshot, I resort to reading Psalms. Weekly is not too often to be with exiles who sat by the river and wept, who went out shouldering their sheaves, who found joy in the morning, had mouths as dry as potsherds, or sheltered under angel wings.

Singing was a welcome distraction. Cadence and accompaniment let me slide over verses that jarred the egalitarian casements of my conscience. Other verses honestly rejoice in all the variety of my human circumference. Joy from my voice is welcome. In spite of the lift of psalms and music, I leave church feeling oppressed. There is no affection for free thought or honest self-examination at First Congregational. Appearance is all religion requires. The immediacy of experience is untouched.

Do we return to our dwellings more patient, not vapid? More peaceful, not complacent? With more self-restraint, not self-indulgent?

The ritual is performed as if life itself were at stake. An obedience to the Puritan taproot. Congregants, not wishing to risk damnation or even a disapproving frown, pay for and warm their pew.

The pressure to be saved had an opposing effect on me. I stopped attendance. Father's and Vinnie's supplications fell hard but not convincingly on my unheeding ears. Their concern for me was sincere but tinged I think with a fear that I might be right. Cracks might spread across the veneer of their certainty.

In my later years, I left the wheedling entreaties to be carried on the willing backs of the religious. Young and old. My soul, I let sing on a different clef. My view of the Bible as an arid document written by faded men faced with the threat of holy specters gentled into respect for its tempting orations, journeys, joys, and triumphs of healing.

September 20, 2007

Well Emily, I too find the prospect of religion to be cringe-worthy. I am saddened by its struggle for relevance. I think we both looked for the deep wisdom experience of Mystery only to chase its disappearing coat tails among revivalists in your case and competing one-note conservatives, and cultural self-help options in mine. Fostering deep wisdom is not on the hierarchical wish list. Myself, I'm not much tempted by weekly rote rehearsals. I have lingering support for the rituals of the hatched, matched, and dispatched majority. Great celebrations of life are made greater in the company of witnesses.

The religious carrot that used to dangle before me was the promise of wholeness as a stand-in for connection missing in family and work. I know well the coy attraction of historic buildings home to equally historic services—the cadence of centuries crowded with gender bias and rules for belonging that roar in my ears—then made deaf by mindless repetition. The brittle language of exclusion is a paradoxic placeholder. People tolerate it though it's far removed from the experience of the Other.

Even with female clergy, divorce, remarriage or no marriage, and attempts at inclusion, cultural apple-carts have been upset from here to the horizon. Our emotional connections and loyalties fray beyond recognition. In a western culture renowned for self-absorption and materialism, the ways that I read, watch TV, telephone, bank, shop, eat and exercise are vastly different from the ways of the first half of my life. Developers and marketers strew their wares across continents with us at their mercy. Institutional religion is one more supplicant wanting time and money.

Appearances are magnified beyond what you might have imagined, Emily. Progress has been made since your day in some respects. Individual choices about work and mates are expected. But we eat too much and work too much to earn not enough. And now that we have language and emotional openness to do so, we spend precious little time with each other. Not caring for ourselves means that neighbors get even shorter shrift. We do not have even the pressure of duty prodding us to action.

Among my aging crowd most would admit publicly that appearances are not of ultimate importance. But we do have large dread and small interest in the fearless self-examination that lurks at the edge of appearance. Approach to the edge is seldom voluntary. First, the thin cover of appearance rips during turning points like death, divorce, job loss, marriage, and birth. We find ourselves in one of my wells where we stay until insight offers a way out.

If our power structure engaged in serious self-examination, there could be startling improvements in social and environmental conditions. But most of the power structure takes advantage by privilege rather than leading by example. Even the Bible, that bastion of male power, is full of leaders who thwart leadership even when asked, we are to believe, by God. Few want the task of guide on the moral and ethical high road where long vision and sacrifice rear their heads. The feel-good road of least resistance and obese egos has riveting appeal.

Enthusiasm for leading, in our modern era, is hampered by the fact that we still kill or fire people who tell the truth and stir fervor for change, for inclusion, for the common good.

Emily, when you met hypocrisy at church, you refused to participate, preferring your cathedral of forest and bird. I can see you under green pastoral arms of pine but what I dream about is a small circle of people who gather. People who are willing to be part of a covenanted group, for a long or short time, to sit in silence, maybe also pray, maybe sing, maybe meditate—to 'see' each other and listen to tales of how we are. Someone I used to know could be counted on to ask "Any G-o-d sightings this week?" Of course, I would remove the G-word and slip in a variant, my current favorites being Divine Reality or the Great Goodness. But I am open to names that do not register as male. I believe my small group would stand present to the reality of Otherness and to one another as channels through which radiate the high-frequency vibe of all things positive. When I visualize a group, I'm curious about what might emerge. Intentional communities? Social hubs? Seasonal and/or liturgical re-enactments? New kinds of reflective, topical gatherings?

My own transformation is not dependent on any particular gathering or institution. The cathedral of forest and bird is open for me as well as the voice of water, a grandchild's smile, or a book. Each equally liable to open my mind to the Mystery and the moment. I could as easily self-identify as agnostic or atheist or humanist and my soapbox ethic of care for self and neighbor through attachment to Mystery would not change. My experience of the holy is internal and deepens in proportion to my ability to ask the universe to show me how to heal and how to welcome my place in the world around me.

Rilke, you wondered
who among angels would hear
if you cried out
into a hollow universe?

I hope you did—cry out,
a cry that careened around stony castle corners.
I do—cry out,
in a car, confining shrillness in cradling metal.

But Rilke, did it work?
Wait—you wrote that you swallowed
the call-note of your dark sobbing—no—
no—don't—
space freed by cries is fruitful
full of longing for the whole.

Along side criers-out
the deads you sensed gather
to send glints of solace
so we know their void
is only unknown
not empty.

November 18, 1884

LIGHT COMES LATER AND LATER. IT HAS SILVERED THE PANES
with sufficient glow for me to see that the words in my head are
the same as the ones I put on paper. As I write, I am consumed by
images of death. They ambush my sensibilities whenever thought
veers away from the day's details. My newly adopted sentences are
more like stones over which I must pass toward a less craggy state
of mind. My heart is calloused brutishly. That it continues at all
under an avalanche of death is a mystery. At least to pray is left.
Oh, Jesus-in the air, I'm knocking everywhere, hast thou no arm
for me?

The glow of day's round sun diminishes through square
windows. Its movement leaves shrunken shadows that mingle
to make dark. The light of heaven has traversed my floor while
I am unmoving in my bed. Death, a close friend of dark, has
called all too frequently. The first of my friends to grieve me so
was my tutor Ben, who died in 1853. Ben, whose every attention
to me and my poetry bolstered my tendency to think thoughts
of independence, of being a professional woman, a poet. Ben's
learnedness, his promotion of my writing talent, his nearness
caused my heart to skip and dance along with intriguing shivers
in my thighs. I cherished a fond eagerness for a future with Ben.
But I was young. Father did not account for a tutor as much
above a servant. There was no utility in Ben pressing his suit. He
moved away, married another, and lived happily until he fell ill
and found death stopping for him after a mere thirty-two years.

I was twenty-three. His death struck me deeply as the vistas of adulthood beckoned. My quick, facile response to the world shrank in sympathy and never quite returned from this brush with the initial shadowy leer of mortality.

The next death was Father. He died in Boston in 1874. He was buried in Amherst. My absence, conspicuous or not, was certain. His demise ushered in a version of vitality for me.

In 1882, Mother died. Even after years of illness, it was unexpected. She flew like one nearing home after long absence. Vinnie and I spent hours caring. Eventually, at least, there was care among the tasks of invalid assistance. Mother needed only to sigh and Vinnie who was the more brave and faithful never let those sighs go unheeded. Vinnie, the diligent in duty, untroubled by aspiration, accepting of her lot. While Mother was bedridden, I thought, wryly, that affection is not guaranteed increase or continuance by virtue of illness or death. Though I do not doubt that the thorns of our connection were clipped from the stem by the mellowing influence of infirmity. We each inclined to be more gracious about our separateness.

As trees welcome their tenants, so that same year did heaven receive my dear sweet hope. Charles. My Philadelphia passed from earth—leaving a bitter raven black pall. Charles. I will write more about Charles. His passing engulfed a secret repression that my kindred spirit and I would meet in light during our earthly sojourn.

My darling nephew Gilbert was eight when he was taken by typhoid the next year. Waves of paralysis seized me in a sea that submerged me again and again. I felt like a puppet whose unseen master jerked my arms and legs in motion. Breathing hurt. For weeks, my heart was marble cold in my chest. No one in the family climbed successfully from the devastation. It was an ogre spreading malevolence throughout my circumference.

This year heart failure robbed us of Judge Otis, Father's colleague, and our long-time family friend. He was my unwavering supporter and recipient of my letters. Our correspondence was packed with the currency of philosophy, humor, and anecdotes of our happenings. Our letters increased in number and depth after the death of his wife. Our late love bloomed with gaudy discretion. His death at the end of a long procession of loss pushed me beyond endurance—my own spirit tripped—fell down and down—to lie crushed by the boots of lead wandering across the surface of my visible life.

This litany of loss visits and long outstays its welcome. Untimely deaths, like my Charles and Gilbert, have clawed raw holes in my soul. The passing Calvary of others paraded behind my eyes with at least a reflection of light. Nonetheless, death has left chasms I must step over to enter each day. Savagely alone, I must keep ahead of the spreading abyss which does not yet afford me the privilege of escape.

The physician says I have nervous prostration—possibly I have—I do not know the name of the sickness that stole my equilibrium and left me cornered, bereft of wider vistas. My bones seemed to crumple, refusing to carry my flesh and thought. The spareness fissured my heart and shortened my breath to sighs and timid sips. I sought steady air as I leaned against reality around me. My limbs felt disembodied. Tears kept my eyes from exploding inside my head. Resources of air and gravity were taxed to keep me upright and ambulatory. Lucidity sat like anvils on my shoulders.

One consolation was my kinship with the departed. In their presence, I was severed for the space of moments, adrift from the universe of time. Function was interrupted during these short amputations of spirit. In this gap, I devoted the minutes of deferred coping to wish goodness to my beloveds gone home. They left a little of their paradise with me when I began anew to cause air currents by movement. Calm settled somewhat in my blackness. Stiffness in my back and small inhalations made me aware again of a hard floor underfoot and a chair compressed against my spine with bruising pressure. Once fully returned to the present time, I found I needed a handkerchief, or felt internal twitches which reminded me of meals not taken.

I could not survive on the thin gruel of death. It was taking my soul—nothing was there to fatten it with joy. Charles, my sweet hope, had been a plump slice of joy. As long as he was alive, teasing his congregation into deeper understanding of Divine experience, I held faint hope that he might come to me. His death collapsed my house of spiritual cards. Subsequent deaths ground the cards to powder. Only grinding reality remains.

Prior satisfactions sent out tentative fingers to tempt my association—although the prospect of tea and my lovely, light bread with jam, or maybe cake crammed with currants and nuts, or a turn around the garden offered no more than momentary respite. Like a cart-horse leaning into a heavy load, the drag of grief pulled me in from all angles. It squinted at me from behind the sugar basin. It drifted with the dust balls under my bed. It grinned from the black ooze of frozen garden plants. It lounged in smug clouds covering the sun.

Even so, in the midst of enveloping gloom, a moment of diversion might brighten my day. A twinge of old wholeness, like flowers, clean linen, or a clear turn of phrase—winked—let me know that I was not abandoned entirely.

November 24, 1884

Writing about the deaths that sit so heavily tempers their effect. The transfer of sorrow to the page permits a measure of composure for mind and body. A glimpse of the gardens or a small household task completed also spreads cracks through my mourning so that gobbets of grief drop throughout the house. Thinly spread for easy absorption.

Charles is the beginning death. Charles is significant. When I traveled home from Washington with Vinnie and Father in 1855, we visited relatives and friends in Philadelphia. While there, I did not object to attending a church service led by the prominent preacher, Charles Wadsworth. I was, in fact, curious to see if he could dislodge my entrenched antipathy for the religious exhortations of First Church.

When I met this preacher, I was twenty-five. Past the usual age for marriage and secure in the establishment of my life pattern. Spousal aspirations loitered lamely but thus far no one had found me. That Sunday I was concerned only that we find seats affording clear sight and sound.

A guileless visit to his church became a baptism. I was baptized before without choice but this time I submitted consciously to the grace of his words. Words that had flown around the universe looking for a mouth that paused long enough to speak them at the right time. A warm recognition rushed over me as of one deep calling to another. An ancient link sailed a line in my direction and I caught hold.

Charles' anecdotes and spiritual quotations addressed reason and feeling. These were not the dry crusts of entreaty at the center of my disaffection with First Church. I had cast those notions aside in favor of inner stirrings that made my heart alive to my own experience of the Holy. I felt a Divinity that formed words in my head and tightened my heart with fervor. Charles preached divine and human alignment. He asked us to take Jesus' habits into the actions of our own days. I heard that I should bask in them each moment and focus on myself, not selfishly, but enough to draw the Holy into my decisions and thoughts. To calm myself with the Holy.

September 25, 2007

creedal statements spread
like official disease
caught through contact
with patriarchal dictate

distance from the infecting group
halts disease progress
but memory pocks
are permanent signs
of its visitation

sweet fruits of self-knowledge
are the replacement disease caught
in quiet and reflection
sweet fruits free me to merge
with a spirit of seeking
among emerging strains
of creedal disease

November 27, 1884

CHARLES, LIKE JESUS, COUNTED THE LIVES AND MINDS OF
women as crucial to civilization's march. When I heard this, I felt
as if a hand reached gently into my chest and squeezed my heart.
My breathing quickened. A shock of assurance shivered through
me as he spoke of the Holy and the human. He seemed alive with
the very idea. Audacity let me believe that I was too.

Though Charles did not greet followers after a service,
I insinuated myself and stammered praise for his preaching.
My impudent eyes would not stop staring into his face. The
tremulous thighs and thumping heart occasioned by Ben had
hinted warmly at the way of men and women. And there it was
again—with Charles. He asked if I would like to talk further.
Unhesitating assent was my reply. Attraction flooded our emotion
and talk flowed without restraint.

So began a conversation that took me prisoner and
released me, changed, hours later. Kindred spirits, indeed. A
thankful blindness kept me from knowing that for each ecstatic
instant, I would an anguish pay. For each beloved hour, coffers
heaped with tears!

His fervor and eloquence were not of this world. He spoke
of the call of the Spirit and The Bride. The call to take the water of
life freely. His adoration of the Holy was humble and penetrating.
Only much scouring by mental conflict, exhaustive travails in
gardens of darkness could produce such confident intimacy with
the Divine. I felt on familiar ground.

He understood how the strictures of First Church placed
an unkind constraint on my spirit. I tried to attend in the face
of Father's and Vinnie's cajoling. But my spirit was oppressed for
days after I ventured a visit. I could not be among mechanical
supplicants who shed Holy ideas before they got anywhere
near their thoughts, never mind changing their hearts. The
congregation formed in a tight submission dulled by stasis.
Charles knew, as did I, that when Jesus was perceived as God, we
turn away. This is not attainable, but when Jesus talked of earth
and broken hearts acquainted with grief, He had us rapt in every
second. Before Charles, I only dreamed of such shared vision.
It was harrowing and of no help to know that God understood
even if my companions did not. Into this gloom, a clergyman
in knightly fashion scaled the wall of my heart and fastened my
colors to his sleeve for eternity.

We walked, hoping to dispel the tension that threatened
to fasten more than our eyes upon each other. I remember
with delight that—where a rose did caper on my cheek, my
bodice rose and fell—till opposite, I spied a cheek that bore
another rose and a vest that like my bodice danced. Walking
only brought us to a handy grove that sheltered more discovery.
Evening shadows protected my foray into the unexplored plot of
night's promise. My memory was numinously etched by pressed
moments through clothes. Our bodies seemed larger, swollen
with unexpressed ardor. I remember my racing breath, a cloudy
blurring of vision. A foggy cloth covered my heart pounding and
lungs drowning for air. No need to remove clothes. Naked souls
shone and flashed with clarity like a firefly's flitting illumination.
Relationship consummated in commingled depth.

The intimacy of our speech, our close communion, never
repeated in my life. Past midnight, past the morning star, what
leagues there were between our feet and day.

I hold secure the remnants of our conversation, but more I
recall the sense of occasion. We hurried over the parched ground
of formal religion to the graciousness of The Comforter whose
presence we knew. Each of us stayed minutely attuned to where

we were—the hard ground softened by grass beneath our feet, light and shadow dappling from trees, bird sound, and wind—while a concert of joy and acceptance was ours to attend.

Matters of routine were not outside our consideration. What is a tithe? Can we tithe spirit? Can we allow that the sacrifice of God is a contrite heart?

Not offerings, burnt or otherwise. He spoke of how he sought to have hearers amend their lives. We mused over what Biblical interpretations suited daily reverence and relevance. Is following the Ten Commandments sufficient? Are good works? Is simply asking to have a rough path made straight enough? Is the point of church attendance to create a fertile ground for transformation?

My belief is that such enlightenment, a Divine link, may occur as readily in a garden or cellar or bed during a wakeful night. And what of training children? Would they absorb morality and civil behavior under watchful parental eyes? Are the eyes of a church community also needed? In any event, they will do what adults around them do. Most of them forever, but some will be hounded off that path by flares of consciousness. Little trips to other realms.

Charles was elated to find a woman like-minded companion. Never had he dreamed of encountering such. A woman who valued prayer and preaching as much as procreation was a true boon. Had we met sooner, we might have married. Surely Father's standard would have been met. Moored in each other—our spirits would soar. Rowing together, we would pass through our tests of suffering and create a life work by reaching back for following spirits facing theirs. Never have I met a man or woman whose expression stayed so alive when forced into the narrowness of words. Words played and released themselves into air between us and later played onto our paper exchanges.

Charles was a married man with children. I knew that. It was a natural choice made long before our meeting. He would continue with this duty as society demanded. His body belonged to the estate of marriage—but his soul had become part of mine. Unlike John Donne's lovers, our souls communed, were consecrated by contact, but declined the physical. Still, those hours then and now admitted me to the plane of belonging. It raced to me, blissfully welcome. I visit that spot again and again from the shelter of my circumference. To cover the distance between us, we wrote with the agreement that letters not be shared with others.

After Father's steady refusals, with my twenty-fifth birthday well behind me and my professional hopes not yet dashed, I began to know that marriage was unlikely. But I had found a point of reference for a relationship. A standard had been set. Having been so stirred, I could never settle for less. No substitute compared. A tempestuous bud of youth had flowered. I found I could live comfortably with my touchstone and my hope—in the absence of the material reality.

Years later, when I could remember Charles with my equilibrium unruffled by inner cataclysms, I wondered about my rigorous standard. Others have their own version of standards. I may have been part of the small cabal that pushed Sue toward marriage to Austin so he would not leave Amherst for adventures in the West. Austin had married Sue and stayed in Amherst bowed by the pressure of tradition and family clannishness. Even the lordly male can be trapped by domestic arrangements. In the face of Sue's vicious swings of temper and crippling fear of childbirth, it was not surprising that Austin fell into a deep and abiding love for Mabel. Austin and Mabel frequently contrived to cross paths. Mabel was tremendous fun, vivacious and lovely. And nearly a professional woman into the bargain. How well I understood the marriage of true minds. How dispiriting for Charles and me that only our minds could be married.

Yearning for like minds lived in me vigorously after I met Charles. It sat on a branch in my mind like a hungry hatchling. Never satisfied, more importunate than the shrill intrusion of the most raucous, early rising birds. Every day for a long while meant rising alone to tread a curvy track of unavailing hope. Duty was a glad and faithful lifeline of endless length, with many loops for grasping. Duty and my calm demeanor hid the volcano within.

I had been writing some few things for a time. I began to share poems and letters with Austin and Sue. Lava channeled safely into words.

September 30, 2007

OH, EM, WHEN I AM CONVINCED THAT I CAN DO WITHOUT SOME material reality, I'm likely deceiving myself. Only wishing I could do without. The wished away, be it car, house, relationship, friends, disease, even my thinner body of yore, assumes a life of its own. Ready to shoot up through the floorboards of my mind the moment I believe I have conquered its nag. When it pokes up at full throttle, I find myself defensive, "Oh, this old thing? I haven't thought about it in years. How odd that it's been lying in my mind's closet all this time." If I genuinely want my space back, what should I do with this apparition of wished away reality—the car, the house, and so on through the litany?

Conquering is not possible. Tenuous suppression is. I never forget. The wished-away is like zebra mussels or buckthorn. Eventually, the patient work of checking the invasion has to be done. I can not simply hack out what has imprinted itself into my memory. Acknowledging the wished-aways is a smart beginning. "Oh, you again!" Then I can begin to make friends with missing realities.

In the end, Emily and I can do without what we perceive to be our particular missing pieces of realities—at the end of hard-won mental and spiritual adjustments. Repeated adjustments until the intrusive sadness or distress that comes with loss can be eased by holding hands with the original hope until the sting fades into a memory I don't mind having. One of my favorite reformed memories that required years of hand-holding remedy, is my need to be rescued—always the helped, never the helper.

My wished-aways eventually recede into their quiet half-life in the back of my mental closet. Happy to be memory and a part of enlarging wholeness that keeps one footstep following another.

November 29, 1884

THE SUN IS WARMING WRITING TOOLS AS THEY WAIT TO WORK.
Sun works too, to penetrate the air chilled by fall. My tools will
transfer warmth to my fingers whose movement will put them
to use. A thick mantle is pulled tightly around my shoulders. My
feet are tucked under my skirt like two sheltering toads. The hard
curve of my chair presses woodenly into my back. For a minute I
will take a seat on my parlor perch of the past.

For girl children, our help was presumed when it was time
to wait upon guests. I was drawn to the parlor where news of
the neighbors and the world was freely dispensed. More so if
callers were Father or Austin's colleagues. They brought tidings
of the state's business affairs, town planning, the war, and a juicy
dissection of oratorial offerings from speakers in town of late
who held forth on topics of current appeal. I was not averse to
news of betrothals, births, recipes, and fashion that came by way
of female callers. Words were as sustaining as the victuals whose
preparation I shirked when I crept down the hall or stairs to
listen. This trick of listening unobserved began as an amusement
and became a practice from which I was an overlooked ear.

Our parlor held a Chinese screen elegant with the grace
of cranes and golden of color. Rigid, black enameled panels
framed an austere landscape, softened by gray mist through
which peeped bits of red on cranes and bright spikes of bamboo.
From this coign of vantage, I perched on a chair. An occasional
nest from which to listen minus the necessity of interchange. I

could follow my wandering notions without adding my 'superior' thought that fought with fussy female chatter despite the fact that the conversation of Father's visitors frequently put my conceit on notice with its traffic in realities of Amherst and far beyond.

The bottom of the screen was a narrow space above the floor. That may be how visitors espied a betraying bit of skirt even if I put my feet on the chair rails. My perch was known to exist. I grant a perception of oddity in the service of collecting words and impressions. Words came to me unexpectedly and would not be denied. Memory kept them until paper did. Since it would be bad manners to take hasty leave of visitors to record images, I took to not entering the main parlor at all. Like many expediencies, it led to established habit.

I listen best when I can take little words gifts and open them in my mind without worry. The ideas I heard dissolved among my own. They enriched the mixture. I know fertility of mind if not of body. I stir in the daily orthodoxies observed by many and create my own. My perch, my simple garb, and solitary hours are freely at the service of my mind. My heart wells up with pen in hand. I briefly control my own expression—it is not at the beck and call of social convention—it is a small power of choice.

November 23, 2007

PERHAPS WE ALL CARRY A HEART IMAGE OF A ROMANTIC
other. Our best hope. It lives buried in its synaptic sepulcher
until the eye of the heart is triggered by another's answering
synapse. Two men have affected me much as Charles affected
Emily. It is a rare occasion when an ancient filament of kinship
arcs between two hearts.

When I was twentyish and my energy was expended by the
effort to stay afloat in the slough of excrescence behind my visual
physicality—I met a man at a wedding. From first encounter, the
artless heart of youth wobbled warmly between whether or not
he might notice me enough to pursue. He did pursue. After post-
wedding let down, after a wild dance in a bright, public fountain
and a late-night drive-through meal, we resumed our separate
realities. Correspondence and care packages followed for a few
months. With no forewarning during my one visit, he announced
that he was moving to India. The lush excitement of our time
together disintegrated. I was crushed by such distance and the
sure knowledge that I could not develop the skills and raise the
money needed to join him.

While I explored the training program for India, I met the
man who agreed to marry me. With the hindsight of forty years,
I realize that there was no hint of heart-twitching charm. But
how did my brain know that he would not interfere with my false
front of function? We married.

Forget apologies, my consciousness did not extend so far as to even tell wedding man who was marking time for me so far away. I met him one more time some months later. His anger and confusion were like a door slammed on my fingers.

He did marry someone else after nearly dying from hepatitis in India. He had a son. Like my own relationship, his did not last—the son and his mother returned to the States—and wedding man went to a home country where he limped toward death from liver cancer.

He was the first man I knew I had hurt by the robotic trap door of my disconnection.

The second man blipped onto my radar two decades later. I felt a jolt of recognition before we actually met. I watched him walk across a field. Grassy hummocks valiantly held their ground among compacted patches of dusty beige dirt. He stooped slightly to push a short-handled stroller that held a babe wearing a white onesie patterned with pink and green spriggy bits. A sun hat shielded the face lolled over one shoulder. Plump arms and legs flopped softly in the stillness of sleep undisturbed by uneven ground.

At the sound of his voice, a cousin of Emily's ancient link flipped into action. My heart bellowed like a calf. And was just as quickly quelled. Like Charles, this too was a married man busy adapting to parenthood and work.

Reflecting on that meeting, I remember a fragment of shame. I had been divorced for ten years. All my resources were contentedly at the disposal of my growing girls. I had excused myself from the relationship arena. As taken aback as I was meeting him, I see now that my best sublimation efforts could not be expected to tamp down curious natural feelings that had never developed to the point of reasonable expression. I was shriven by the shining link and my warm involuntary response, then made a mental note to pay more attention to that part of my life.

December 2, 1884

Happy laughter carrying far in the cold drew me to the window. Two boys were tugging a sleigh burdened with wafting fronds of pine. Pine separated from its source, destined to give its remaining green for a brief Christmas display.

The red-cheeked boys robbed my breath. I sat down hard, the edge of my bed groaned with my weight scarcely louder than my moan in memory of Gilbert. It was an unguarded moment. My shield must have been off for polishing. I felt like a bird hopped away from its nest's surrounding security. I saw Gil's face for the space of a breath. I froze in imitation of the paralysis of being that hurricaned through the house with the word of his death.

Strained sunshine had scampered through his veins—arms and legs did battle with air—he breathes so air wins. His "done up in dimples" temperament lent assurance that he had a little of me in him. Alongside his own cheery disposition and his chirping child's voice, he discovered that his speech magnetized people around him. He did not have the sour, self-interest of his mother, Sue, but exhibited the curiosity and wit of his Dickinson side. He brought balm between sparring factions in the family.

He gave me many occasions to visit the club for mothers. I did not belong to this club and most days did not want to, but to hold Gilbert, read to Gilbert, help who he was emerge was a pulsing, delicious taste of the motherhood club. Often, after he went home, I ached to belong to the club. I learned to befriend this ache as it gave every sign of being permanent, as I had learned to shelter all such aches of absence like children and the means of their creation.

I admit the soft impeachment of selling a piece of my soul in my attachment to Gilbert. His death was an amputation without ether. His sweet command in delirium, "Open the door, open the door, they are waiting for me . . ." is consolation that when released from fevered anguish, he met comfort. I would give much to know the energy, the quality of light that he recognized when he went through the door and fled to welcome.

When the dire news came from the house next door, I sat down hard. Though I have never been aboard a ship, the floor heaved under me rolling and ebbing as would the sea. The horizon twisted—I could not be sure when my feet would hit the floor—the village drunk was far surpassed by my swaying, groping for purchase movements—as if the floor had turned to ice. For days sure footing was a memory. The thought that I would have to bear this seemed absurd. The absence of his special reality was surely unsurvivable. My well of grief was dry—not a drop of sustenance to be had.

Today, as I sit, with the old sensations blown past, a new feeling is left behind. The Divine and the human have struck a harmony. The Divine has me for a clay partner and I have the Divine making my blood dance with certainty that Gilbert will come for me. As will Charles.

With each remembrance of Gil, my body seems lighter—a glow shimmers through my skin. Vinnie will ask if I have done my hair up differently. My appearance alters. I am changed. My sentences have made a donation as well. What was sealed away is opened and spread on the page. Leaving space in my mind. For an embrace of the immediate with no fear that gorgons of old despair will drag me in their wake.

November 30, 2007

IF I HAD BEEN SITTING WITH YOU EMILY, INSTINCTIVELY I WOULD
have put my arm around your shoulder, or held your hand—
feeble but human efforts to console amid the disorientation and
vulnerability after a shock. I have would stayed until rigid aching
tension diminished.

Since I was not there, I am glad you had the Divine, with
its ever-present inclination to engage the apparatus of resilience,
at that time and as you lived your last three years. Good feeling,
however small, irrespective of circumstances is a sure sign of
that loss being integrated. But I grant that losing Gilbert was
to lose the glory of watching him unfold, to lose the promise
of easier relations among family members, to lose the promise
of continuity that children represent, and to be forced into
acquaintance with precarious existence—not in our control.

worms of spring—for Gilbert—
fecund mother
earth disgorging
Prematurely

pale strings
surprised by spring
frozen
from an earthy retreat

incongruous mother
earth creating
the sweet rain
of spring
that kills

December 10, 1884
My Birthday!

LOSING GIL WAS A PAIN SO UTTER. ALL HE DID WAS BATHE IN the nearby pond. A daily occurrence with a friend during the heavy rays of summer. His friend never ailed a thing, while Gil beside him carried home the virulence of typhoid. Still, I am glad he did exist. And he would not have but for the marriage of Austin and Sue.

How subdued was the reaction to their nuptials. They performed them away from Amherst with none of us present. The marriage took place in Geneva, New York though Sue had not lived there for several years. Each had an air of doing the right thing. When Sue and I were friends before the marriage, Austin favored Sue's sister Martha. She was prettier. A blithe, flirtatious, and sociable young thing. Sympathetic to Austin's opining and philosophizing but her modest capacities did not extend to understanding. She was looking for conventional married life that would keep her orthodox piety intact. Soul-searching, cogitation of deep ideas left her behind.

Sue was living in Amherst while Austin was at law school. She was proximate. She deflected rather than commiserated with his contemplative tangents. She was ambitious and knew that she wanted a settled home from which her status would proceed. An eligible Amherst bachelor was her aim. Austin was eminently eligible. She pressed her case for marriage in spite of the death of one sister in childbirth and the other's previous attachment to Austin. Father also pressured. He wanted Austin to stay in Amherst. To that end, Father built a new house next door. Austin's own uncertainty about his future, the availability of Sue, and his affection for me persuaded him to give up the lure of the western frontier.

There was triumph in Sue over the engagement rather than elation. Social position had been achieved. Later, I understood how much she abhorred conjugal duties and feared childbearing. She was content to have her invitations, her salons the most sought after. And they were. An opulent life and much materiality were cover for what Austin called her ungovernable behavior with family.

Sue and I had giggled during our early friendship, as girls do, over 'married life.' Young women's sole aspiration was to join its elevated status. Identity and all trappings of wifely occupation established by a sweetly nervous exchange of vows. A gulf existed between me and women who embraced the acceptable concealment of self to assist the creation and growth of other-selves. New selves with more potential than the breeding vessel.

I hope in truth that Austin did not use our friendship, our sympathetic connection of temperament as an excuse to not pursue adventure. I hope also that Vinnie was not more ardent in romantic pursuits out of deference to me. She never had the introspective, brooding talents that set me and Austin apart.

I hope she did not compare and find herself wanting. Perhaps I might have been more encouraging of her romantic pursuits. My social graces fell into disrepair. Rents beyond a quick stitch to hem or cuff would have required new pieces of a different design. I did not expend the effort at so extensive a repair. Disinterest and debility derailed any attempt.

Vinnie became the rock. At its most stable in crisis. She sailed around town transacting the family business. Came home laden with shopping and stories about doings in our stolid burg. Her snappish wit made her welcome if a bit formidable among the tongues in town. She was the source of all things Dickinson to its residents and in return gleaned tidbits to stoke our town bound gossip. She did not, mind you, brook one word of criticism of her family. She declaimed so vehemently on our behalf one evening that I sent Maggie to part her and a caller at the door.

Vinnie replaced marriage with loyalty to our family as her calling. A far more graceful response to spinsterhood than my odd retreat. She ironed sheets and seemed not to dream about sharing them.

Vinnie was shepherd for the routine of service that kept the appearance of a smoothly functioning household. It was smooth to large degree. The war was between the houses, not within the house.

Our spinster selves coexist. With my moment of brocade and crown of wife denied—my garments impart the prickly sackcloth irritation of undeserved atonement. Vinnie and I spun our separate threads. Knitting together days and colors of seasons.

January 20, 1885
Morning

SNOW CURLS DOWN TODAY AND KEEPS EVERYONE IN. EVEN OUR winter paths, worn by contingency, are silent and without walkers. Confined to bed, I wander the paths via imagination. I fondly recall days when a bare-headed sun nurtured green and growing things.

How quickly the hours pass when my mind unrolls recollections. I can peer into a scene where the scroll of memory stops. Paths in memory can be traversed without exertion, without shoe leather, without clean clothes, and without company to distract from remembered sensation. Propped in bed, I can at least muster the motion to push pen across paper!

I have a particular fondness for outdoor places that were scenes of childhood romps. Austin, Vinnie, and I played outdoors around our Pleasant Street house. We were north of Main Street, almost out of town. We lived there for fifteen years between 1840 and 1855. The house was large and its location afforded us a small country walk to town. Or an easy carriage ride if we were ill-favored by weather. My bedroom window overlooked the cemetery. I had ample opportunity to muse over the lives, many of them Dickinsons, given in service of Amherst's history.

Our gardens were near woods, fields, and ponds. From first hints of crocus cleaving through cold to brittle crusty leaves in little dry heaps, we roamed through our domain.

Outside, we hid from each other, gazed at clouds, and played running games until springy earth was forced and formed into flatness by our thousand running steps. Permanent furrows formed summer tracks, ready for our races. These were accomplished far enough away from the house so that Mother and Father could not see me or Vinnie climb or run. Not only was such activity unbecoming, but dampness and stray breezes would surely be blamed for summoning some sickness or other. Propriety was exacted even from the young. But who could still the exuberance in our legs and arms? Who would defraud a bird of its song?

Vinnie and I took off our pinafores and hung them on tree branches. We called them our pinaforests. We took them off because the dark color of everyday clothes told fewer tales of our rambles. Bits of bark from climbing or grass smears disappeared into the fabric and refused to reveal the day's secrets. Prim pinnies were always in place at home, though Vinnie might glance out the window before reaching for hers as if pinnies naturally grew on trees.

I liked hide and seek. Letting the environs absorb me. I felt like a thief, stealing time and invisibility. Or a prisoner lying down to peek through blades of grass like bars of a cell between me and sky. From my hiding spots, colors, aromatic winds, plants, birdsong, insect hum, and earth texture seemed meant only for me. Their vitality accepted mine among a community of created things as I crouched and waited to be found. I would much rather hide than be seeker.

At mealtime, scratches and scuffles receded behind the veneer of pinafores. Our quandaries, confusions, and explorations subdued for another day. We arranged ourselves properly for home. Curiosity, play, woods, fences, and berries growing beyond—all shielded by white cotton.

January 20, 1885

Later

PATHS AND OUTDOOR ADVENTURES STILL OCCUPY MY MIND.
They did not disappear entirely with childhood. A few times at
night, during the middle of my life, when the purveyors of sleep
passed me by, I took it upon myself to try and do their job. When
my body lay unbending in bed, clenched and ready to crack, I
went out to find the respite from unbending offered by darkness.

No night thief or mischievous urchin was quieter. Barefoot
down the stairs, easing over steps that protested my presence.
Hurriedly, over my white nightdress went a dark cloak. Then
shoes, never mind hose. Through the back door. The cold latch
giving way slowly in my grip. Out the well-oiled door, kept so to
prevent unseemly broadcast of the numerous ins and outs of our
daily round.

Once in the garden, I looked for lights as neighbors also
may be passed over by the sleep purveyors. But on my nights 'out'
the only light was a few friendly moonbeams. Familiarity was an
easy path to follow. I made for the fields nearby and raced into
rows. Back and forth, I ran or trotted, holding close my cloak
so as not to flash my pale cotton. Back and forth, with my neck
bent back trailing silent screams that made my throat ache. Soon
my legs refused to go farther. I sank onto my knees, choked for
breath. My lungs, like a surprised wife, hurried to open doors to
give sustaining space to unexpected guests.

The way home was a quiet march indeed—still cautious—surely anyone watching would have marked the stilted gait and wondered with concern what sort of apparition was abroad. The stiltedness would continue to force itself on me for a day or two after such unaccustomed movement. On the night, my limbs returned home ready to rest. Thankfully, they lulled my mind to rest as well. Sleep then performed its restorative act.

In winter, pacing replaced the head-long run, though not so effectively. Fists beating air and feet trying not to attract notice take more time to tire. Thankfully I was never caught with my neck arched back or my face contorted like a grimacing gargoyle—an arresting sight that would have been. I might well have been accused of something worse than a penchant for solitude. Confinement rebels against itself. It is good that calming the mind's clamor can be accomplished with or without the body's help.

Such episodes earned the attention of the sleep purveyors, reminding them of guilty neglect. They would stay on the job for weeks before becoming neglectful again, leaving me to slake my tiny night 'madness.' On occasion, my body demanded a response during the day. The result was gape-mouthed, silent screaming, my forehead smacking gently the nearest wall or tree, fists flailing, knees locked until tension was absorbed into the surface conveniently at hand. A brisk, daylight walk to the shops or even beyond the yard, I could not do. Conversations might have to be entertained, invitations declined or explanations tendered for my reserve.

Now, my volcanic exuberance is long past. A volcano can never be completely stilled but time has taken agitated physical urgency and replaced it with worthy battles of words. Words surrounded my experience and carried the expression I was denied socially and physically. The volcano was aided by age with its acceptance of limitation and a tandem replacement of fire in the blood with fire in the spirit. Not that my spirit lacked fire, but I did notice a friendly coming to terms between agape and eros. The stability of agape being more sustaining.

A comfortable routine formed. It wore familiar grooves in my spirit. Propriety outweighed other considerations. I prefer my garden and my ink to the nasty rap to my sensibilities when forced to endure the unexamined opinions of my peers.

December 8, 2007

sought a friend
for solace
but find the living
bespoken
so seek instead
among the dead

January 25, 1885

THE SMELL OF FRESH BREAD CLIMBED THE STAIRS, WAFTED
under the door and sidled into my sensibilities as welcome
as a pup. Vinnie is baking. My eyebrows rise in surprise that
her aromas made the trip—my bread being the lighter. Father
remarked on the lightness of my fine white bread. He felt out
of sorts when I was not baking. Would that he rhapsodized so
earnestly over my literary interests. True to his upbringing, he
would have women trained in homemaking arts as well as social
arts to better elicit suitably harmonious conversation. His ideas
of education did not extend to independence for women, not
even independence of thought. Behind the curtains of my brain,
thought traveled its own path.

Bread baking is so nicely practical. Dry, musty-
smelling nuggets of yeast bubble into a foamy pungent puff.
Transformation abetted by a feeding of water and sweet, to form
the fragrant sustenance of bread. Or crust for tarts. Cold butter
chunks absorb sandy grains of sugar—together with powdery
flour as they recompose themselves as crust and dough. A golden
crust on top or a glossy robe of jam glaze. Mother reserved glaze
for special occasions. Plain pie filled with whatever oddments lay
at hand were viewed as treat enough for everyday.

Kneading bread is monotonous. Energy from my arms and
shoulders goes into the dough which after it is baked and imbibed,
returns it back to my body. How interesting—an assortment of

ingredients lose their separate identities to become something new—the newness, in turn, loses its identity becoming me.

It snowed overnight. Then perhaps the damp outside is yeast to the world. Seeds and buds swell, split and seek nourishment from light and air. Gossamer dew dresses the tongues of grass and slicks leaves in summer. Freezing dew creates an elegant fairyland of crystals on window panes in winter. Dense freezing dew thickly rimes every surface with a hoary purity.

Damp is not good for molasses candy. A rare indulgence. Vinnie and I picked cool, dry days for taffy. This was one watched pot that did boil. And boiled until one pearl showed itself brittle in water. Then the careful addition of vinegar, staying well away from its sizzling leaps. Waiting followed until it was cooler. We greased our hands and pulled and looped until a shiny golden snake slithered between us. It was snipped into pieces for passing around and melting in our mouths on the spot. A bit of approved gratification.

Gingerbread announced itself by penetrating every corner with spicy scents of the imported East. Ginger and cinnamon, harbingers of holidays or guests. Small squares on best china topped by a dollop of whipped cream that blandly foiled its volatile tang. Pound cake was deemed a company confection with its extravagance of eggs, butter, and sugar. Pound cake and fruit cake were often stored, soaked in spirits. Mother taught. Vinnie and I copied the tradition of setting a fine table. Community, even of family, shared food together.

January 12, 2008

THE SCENT OF BAKING BREAD HAS BEEN KNOWN TO BRING
people to tears. I believe it. For years I made bread for family
lunches and toast. White bread at first, deferring to daughterly
preference. Then I began to add handfuls of wheat germ or oat
bran to pump up food value. I was pleased that at least the girls
were not getting dough conditioners, additives, or preservatives.
And I had a machine with dough hooks that relieved the tedium
of kneading. Bonus was a consistent result.

In an apartment building, I loved the thought of teasing the
neighbors with the vapors of baking bread as they returned from
errands and work. Scents are said to be most evocative among
the senses. No doubt I caused a few 'remember when' moments
among the other tenants.

We had to eat some still warm slices, slathered with honey
or peanut butter or jam. Extra loaves were double bagged and
frozen. At our rate of use, I baked about every two weeks. I recall
a time when I ran out of homemade bread and purchased a loaf
from the bakery section of a supermarket. One of my girls looked
at her sandwich and said, "Do you expect me to eat this?" The first
reaction, mentally made, "How rude! Make your own lunch then."

My second reaction was, "Well, this is really a compliment.
She recognizes and likes the difference between bought and
homemade, and appreciates my work." In the end, my out-loud
response was something of an apology that we had used all the
homemade, that I would make more on the weekend. I don't think

I even upbraided her for the snippy tone. I wasn't being a complete servant-parent, since I have always baked for my own pleasure and occupation.

Besides bread, I keep an eye open for possible additions to my list of bundt cake recipes. They must be remarkable to make the cut. The chosen few are celebration cakes made to share. With no expense spared, I buy free-range eggs, designer butter, organic extracts, and chocolate, cream, or maybe buttermilk. One favorite has four kinds of chocolate. Another is a lemony, citrus pound cake. Then there is the bundt full of fresh blueberries for summer, followed by a bundt luscious with cinnamon, black walnuts, and zucchini for fall. And that one may be outdone by a carrot cake that is a tender blend of pineapple, coconut, applesauce, and tart orbs of golden raisins.

Cake is a luxury. It absorbs income left after essentials like bright-colored vegetables and protein. I have a fanciful notion that the care I take in-home baking transmits as well-being and gratitude to tasters.

January 30, 1885

THERE IS GREAT COMFORT IN THIS DWELLING. I KNOW HOW THE clock hands crawl. I know the look of window light on the floor. I know what floorboards deliver a confessional creak as I tread to my desk when awakened by words. I place paper to catch them. Here at home my circumference is the universe bounded by four walls but feels wider for wandering than yard or town. And at last, these walls are no longer filled with fear of coming feet or a turning knob's warning.

Dozy cold keeps me in bed longer to anticipate winter morning floors that burn the bottom of my feet with cold. Unlike summer floors that lure as soon as rays of sunbeams lay over my face. Winter light is thin, slit by my blade body as I stab through to stoke the fire. Vinnie and I live in the kitchen most when it is cold. The stove sheltered by walls that shelter us. Mind you, most afternoons the sitting room has a fire in the event guests brave the cold to visit. Vinnie warms the inside of them with tea and cookies or cake. Their conversation is a worn cloth.

From my home, I keep up with the progress of our corner of society. Vinnie's callers bring snippets of village interest. Sadly, their condition of soul, their stretch of mind, even the movement of light are no cause for comment. But my enjoyment of snippets can be marred by too much of such temporality. The humdrum distracts when my mind would rather wander to the deeps, in the shades of light and stillness that bring companionate bits of wholeness.

I have too long been tied to my solitude. While Vinnie
and I have routines, she does the lion's share while I pretty my
mind with creatures and snows and things that grow. I doubt
that Vinnie knows how I spend my time, beyond letters and
why paper and ink require frequent replenishment. Few would
envy me. The structure of my life would seem distasteful. I am
disinclined to account for my shunning.

I wonder if I am a staple of conversation in the shops of
town. Have talkers peopled my life with invented or remembered
suitors? Was Father made to be a tyrant who forbade my being
in town? Do they tell of parties, entertainments where my laugh
was loudest? Are women asking if any has the recipe for my
prize-winning Indian Bread? Would they shun me as a heretic for
not throwing myself on the steps of salvation? I am certain that
many conversational quips were exchanged between yard goods
and tea. I was made a jewel of amusement flashing from the glass
encasements.

Mrs. General Store: "Well, the house help, Maggie, says that
she spends much of her time in her room. But her simple attire
does make for less maintenance. Not that the girls do laundry."

Mrs. Blacksmith: "Her poor sister does the work is what I
heard. Their mother never did crack the whip hand over them.
Now that she is ill, no doubt Emily pleases herself."

Mrs. Pastor: "Let us not be uncharitable. Who knows what
demands are made by the sickbed. They seem very faithful in
their tending. What fortune that neither sister married, though
I heard they lost opportunities by being both too particular and
too accommodating of their father's opinion. Mind you, all's well
that ends well, because now they can devote their time to nursing
and whatever small pursuits can be accomplished while the
mother sleeps."

Mrs. Blacksmith: "I am sure I do not mean to imply that
Emily is a shirker. No one knows. She may be dutiful in the exercise
of her portion of housekeeping. Abstemious too, I believe. I know
that my Mr. Blacksmith enjoys a drop now and again behind the

anvils with a customer, but I would not trade our modest living for the easy purchases made by the Homestead dwellers."

Mrs. Pastor: "Well, my Pastor does not imbibe. It would be unfitting. Miss Dickinson has sought spiritual counsel in the past. I observe those visiting the parish office in the event that tea is desired. I do believe that she is all right in the head, merely willful in her casting aside our dogma. Would you look at the price of flour? And sugar. If this continues, I shall have to bake less. What will Mr. Pastor and the congregation think?"

Mrs. General Store: "Prices are high. Supplies have been hard to come by since the war. I am fortunate that Mr. General Store has plain wants. A hearty pie of mince or apple or a bit of dark cake and he is satisfied. I'm told that Emily gives away much of their baking to passing children. However, are they enticed into her vicinity?"

Mrs. Blacksmith: "Do you ever think of calling?"

Mrs. Pastor: "In truth, I drop by to visit with Miss Lavinia as part of the parish rota, to offer moral support. Miss Dickinson never deigns to appear. And of course, their mother is abed. I hope I know my duty even if their condescension rankles."

My dears, my dears, such weighty matters. My head is full of ponderings. I think I rather favor the practical sip behind the anvils for the present relief of weary toilers from farm and burg. A welcome interval away from the elements. The relentless demands of field and family.

February 17, 1885

BRIGHT DAY BY DAY BECKONED BEFORE I WENT AWAY TO SCHOOL at Mount Holyoke. Days full of promise like friends who link arms to pull each other along. Though not far distant, Mount Holyoke was the end of comradely childhood. After battles with unfamiliars that left me heart-sore for home, I became intrigued by chemistry, physiology, and botany. Literature invigorated with the language and lore of other lives. My delight was large when I entered their precincts to find balm and stimulation.

I was pulled to earth with a bump when Father decided I would not return to Holyoke for the second year. I had only been a little ill in spring. Not sufficiently ill to warrant the end of formal learning. Adulthood was just beginning to inveigle me into a world of ideas worth exploring. Adulthood also loomed with its settledness. I began to know that adult freedom was not free—it came weighted with many and severe curbs and obligations.

At home, learning was regulated with magazines from moral mainstays like *Scribner's* and *Atlantic Monthly* arriving by mail. Books came home with Father from work or by purchase. I had time and patience to listen and dwell a while between their covers. I took kernels like generous gifts to add to the pot I stirred. They thickened into my philosophy. Mother's passive influence never extended into scholarly matters. Father's rigorous but selective worldliness attempted to monitor my exposure, but he was often from home and the library door was not locked.

I can still hear his voice thundering in my ear to quell our sibling loudness or our disregard for his guidance. His dislike of domestic upset was intense. When it occurred I wondered whether I wanted those confines for myself, for a lifetime. Mother met his requirement for tame domesticity. She dropt the playthings of her life—trembled, obeyed, and was silent. A cadence of disagreement drifted through walls laying discourse of civil restraint upon my young ears although no doors slammed.

Father's emphasis on educating me ran alongside Mother's self-effacing and well-traveled track of household management. I saw little equal exchange between them. Housekeeping and childbearing confined her behind the scenes as unobtrusive background on the family stage. Needless to say—she tried to mold me to meekness—to servant status distinguished by marriage.

On the other hand, I might well have tiptoed into the holy estate of matrimony replete with the risks from those little time and sometimes life takers if a noble candidate armored for worthy word battles had charged into the scene. I do not believe that I could purge myself in the manner that Sue frequently sought as it was suspected that Ned's fits resulted from a failed purge. As I observed Sue, Mother, and others of my circumference, I was ably acquainted with the wifely goal of promoting the prominence of a husband who provided hearth and home. It seemed a long road with few digressions or diversions.

Father as remote head of household expected dutiful children. My confusion was large between the lively life of my mind and the limits of homely prospects. Confusion defaulted to duty. Bits of duty clung to my clothes with the insidious ensnarement of burrs. How could I have guessed the eventual result?

From the provocation of mind at Amherst Academy and then Mount Holyoke, there was no turning back. It had been fun to learn, berry pick, to sleigh, make candy, giggle, sing, and gossip. For my chums whose destiny went unchallenged, it was a program of alignment as proper as correct clothing. Before marriage, the daily round of entertaining activities functioned as a platform to exhibit potential wifelyness pending betrothal's onset. After marriage, they would vanish into its realm. I too waited for a time when my heart quickened over the advent of a groom. A groom akin to Austin or Charles—who listened and acknowledged my personhood. Eventually, I ceased to chase after the laws of diminishing returns. Gloom, hard on the heels of my distress, was diminished by books, fledgling poems, and family obligations.

Intriguing and expansive male conversation continued to intrigue me. Father, Austin, and Ben each piqued my curiosity with philosophy and the breadth of goings-on in the world. Action followed ideas for them. No such urbanity for me. It lived far from feminine tittering and speculation about everything male except the mind. I will admit an appealing frisson of something more than fraternal in some of Ben's looks and jokes. Any small tremors in my midriff I covered quickly with conversation. This must be the trick that seduces young women into blessed but timid intimacies with the resulting miracles who inspire years of watchful fear lest their breathing be snatched. I felt certain that such would not flower from the flux of my loins.

I did have had my daily routine. The summons to the day—wanted sometimes more than others. Wanted when dreams haunted me out, then I welcomed morning. Other times I wished to nestle longer, a languid lady of leisure awaiting the arrival of a lady's maid with tea, toast, writing materials, and the vista of a warm bath. A sweet vision whose indolence was its own demise.

Once I was in the day, I shouldered a share of work. I could seldom keep my mind on dirty vegetables, bloody meat, or gray wash-water and powdery scouring substances. There was little mystery in domestic tasks, perhaps not any, except relief from thinking. Most often, my eyes wandered out the window or my feet carried me to the garden.

My friendship with paper and pen was true. My offerings were accepted and never with chiding. My words recorded the roiling in my head. Sometimes what roiled were thought pieces that refused to cohere. Sometimes they arrived in militant formation with no mistaking their meaning. Charles was conversant with this realm of my circumference. My neighbors thought perhaps that I was the one with a narrow life. I had an answer for them. It was simple. Like seeks like, so I did not expect sojourners on my independent path.

I saw mothers hovered together in a haven of safety for children. Fathers exchanged ideas, often with feeling, about control over the 'rules' of politics, of religion, of our encompassed small town. Couples courted. Each generation mined to exhaustion the same conversational veins.

As I lacked the daily addition of neighborly, if unvaried pleasantries, my mind-space filled instead from within. I wrote letters and took congenial comfort from newsy musings I sent to those of my acquaintance. I fissured the atmosphere with my paper zephyrs. Poems became my secret correspondence—a coded attempt to corral anger and pain with civil expression that calmed me. What I did not know was that this secret could make me sick—from entrenched isolation and attempted understanding. But at the start, I foresaw no clouds over the sun as I initiated myself into truth through literacy.

March 7, 2008

TRUTH IN MY ERA IS WHATEVER YOU WANT IT TO BE. EACH OF us finds a toehold in the succession that flashes by through the filters of family and media. We worship before some material reality. True to history, one reality may be conventional worship in the unexamined dogma of a specific denomination. It is a choice made less and less frequently in favor of equally unexamined peer support.

What is it that keeps adherents of a particular denomination adhering? The eternal unanswerables? What is a soul? What animates a life? Do we need any of it? I think we respond to the questions according to our interest and our need. Then we surround ourselves with those who have a similar response. Children are born into that group and adopt its doctrine. Why think for yourself when you can tag onto the thinking of others? Communities hang together based on accepted law and ritual rooted in ethics and morality. It is to be hoped that law and ritual are grounded in inclusion and other goodness.

For me, the presence of otherness has existed as far back as I can remember. The first memory being my spread-eagle falls backward into the neutrality of dissociation. This led to an early sense of encasement in a glass carapace. I looked as if I were an average functionary in my surround, but in fact, I was always a step outside of it.

I had a miserable friend for a while in grade school who led me into a spasmodic spell of shoplifting. Toffee bars after swimming or Barbie clothes. On one occasion with my Barbie outfit stashed in my swim bag—I began to feel breathless—the next thing I knew I was outside the store on the sidewalk waiting for this friend before we fled. My feet fueled by fear and fury at being so helplessly led followed that curious moment of blankness in the Barbie aisle of the store.

A few years later I was with a group of eighth-graders gathered in a backyard igloo hollowed from a snowdrift big enough for the purpose. A flashlight and a bottle were the objects need to play Spin the Bottle. The light showed the spin, the kisser, and the kissee. Then lights out for the kiss. I was more than grateful for darkness when I expected a kiss, but my cheek was slapped instead. Not hard, but sufficient to reinforce my unapproachable status.

My fear of being identified as an interloper let me slink under social radar with unobtrusive civility, in whatever circumstances I found myself. I acted a part. No one mirrored or modeled the heart version of human agency early enough for me to access, so I have muddled on guided by my lived experience. I lived for years, near but not in, supportive human relationship. I was unaware of the value of my existence. I also lived with a hopeful hunch that re-framing could happen and that it would be slow. Truly Em—the truth must dazzle gradually, with many returns to old adaptions, so the ground of my being would be prepared for re-engagement with my world.

The glass carapace of survival cracked eventually under the halting onslaught of positive feelings. The crack crept at a pace that let me savor small pleasures without being swamped. I began to contribute during meetings, began to assume small leadership roles, and went back to university—twice. Moderation's middle began to hold the balance that emerged between the lively Divine reality in my life and my very human self in the world. The gap I perceived between my public and private personas narrowed. No rote observance required. Nor money, good works, or membership pledges. Merely my presence in the moment.

I can no longer find cheap grace by settling for unstudied ideas or relationships. Study and interaction allow acceptanceof human complexity rather than condescending tolerance in the face of ambiguity. Understanding and adaption test the strength of channels used for compassion and empathy.

Outside the carapace, solitude and silence are now friendly places, not pathological evidence of a misfit. Solitude still recharges me but these days I visit, I don't live there. It feeds fat thinking. I don't want to be materially obese as compensation for an emaciated soul or thin thinking. Not that I am not much threatened by materiality with my hourly income apportioned and gone upon receipt.

As my aura of self-acceptance and its accompanying comfort expand, I am watchful for ego's siren call. It readily confuses self-acceptance with a complacent self-satisfaction in thought or deed. Catching myself, however briefly, in a prideful moment, pushes me—outside of Divine Reality—and ego's knives of anxiety and distrust attack with all manner of drops—stumbles—bumps—forgotten lists, lunches, laundry quarters—ego's effect is similar to a dog's choke collar. I notice this and deliberately return to letting things happen rather than trying to make them happen.

March 22, 1885

CHARLES PAID A VISIT IN 1861. HE SENT NO WORD SO I HAD NOT
the anticipation of it. When Vinnie summoned me, I looked
in the glass and saw my plain muslin house dress, my hair
throttled back into a bun but my face rosy with interest. Between
heartbeats—hope flared—in the same moment I knew that
seconds of hope might not survive past entering the parlor.
Potential and promise entwined for a future in seconds. I am
not sure my feet hit the floor between my room and the parlor.
I would know upon seeing his face. Whatever the outcome,
nothing could diminish the satisfaction of seeing him. Of passing
time in the light of our kinship.

He stepped forward as I entered—hands reaching—my
mind was riven by the warmth of welcome together with a dull-
eyed and slack-shouldered posture that informed of his coming
to me—not his coming for me. Alas. After a long, tight clasp,
manners rescued me. I asked him to sit and bustled off to the
kitchen to arrange tea and cake.

Social tension dissipated through the orderly taking of tea.
Then he craved the boon of a walk down the lane toward the
country. Even the blustery, sobbing winds of March could not
cool our rekindled conversation. Each sounding out the depth
of our long-distance connection. We walked out and away from
the eyes of town to where a hand could be held without scrutiny.
To where only grass and trees were witness to a long embrace.
I refused to use so short a time for tears. But to etch his every

feature into my mind, to commit his every word to memory. I put away all thought of leaden hours to come.

Streaky sunbeams webbed our walk. Brave green was forcing its way through cold clods. Pale purple and yellow spears of crocus busily renewed the life held in the dark of their fleshy corms. The wild freshening breeze was blowing leaves into being before our eyes, even while my heart began to freeze with knowledge that henceforth our shared quarters would continue to be among the dominions of cloud. Our relationship must breathe through the mystery of ink pulled into proscribed shapes to convey detail and meaning.

We spoke of friendship, of enduring affection. How much we have been sustained by the depth of our empathetic spiritual sensitivity. As we strolled, he said that he had spoken obliquely among his colleagues to ascertain on behalf of a 'friend' what might be the likely outcome of divorce. He had been informed that his 'friend' would lose social standing though not so much as his former wife. Wry comment had been made to him, even as a clergyman, that his 'friend' should keep a mistress, with all discretion, if both were desirous.

Charles' 'friend' has all my commiseration. That remedy was surely impractical in our situation unless we trekked west to the developing territories where shredded reputations might not follow or matter. I wonder how the wildlife would react to Charles' magnificent oratory. It would seem a waste of his professional success. Indeed.

Given our mutual comfort in the solitary, and a nod to the honor of selflessness, we could not between us muster the wherewithal to enact that scenario. Our present status makes possible our agreeable lives. Should we take the course of flight, its luminous possibilities might well wear thin under the weight of daily function. The enormous sacrifices made could become an insupportable burden of gratitude for each of us. To say nothing of the darkening thrown onto the souls left behind. Thus we resolved that the scope of our exchanges will be confined to paper.

Charles related that he and his family were being sent to a congregation in San Francisco. It would involve a journey of some weeks around the tip of South America. We will correspond within the frequency permitted by sea miles and in envelopes bare but for the receiver's name. Such cautionary cloaks would shield us from public inspection. I buried for the benefit of herbage or burned his letters, as he did mine after they came apart on the folds from use.

He had learned to discharge doubt and desolation by inscription as I have done. Dark moods, melancholy, as well as heart-tightening seconds of communion were safely removed to paper—not left to prey on his mind. My poems and letters remind him, he says, of the utility of expression and are the dearer for that.

I find comfort risen to the edge of cheer in return. Spiritual dilemmas may resolve or at least become bearable through honest airing to an attentive ear or eye as the case may be. I stated that as I put forward my musings to him. In large measure, this kept my believing lithe.

When he left, I watched him out of sight. A numb recollection flitted through my mind of Elizabeth Barrett Browning who married secretly and eloped to Italy. It returned her to health, brought her a son, and she wrote the glorious saga of *Aurora Leigh*. And then of George Eliot who lived boldly without benefit of marriage with her beloved Mr. Lewes who was only separated from a wife who would not consent to divorce. George was in raptures. She wrote reams. Recollection returned me to the present—Charles was leaving—for a congregation in San Francisco. He would be gone some years.

As he passed from sight, I stayed supported by the gate post. When I willed my legs to walk, they took me upstairs to my bed. Oblivion settled over me in sleep. By morning a phantasm quality would be all that remained of our happy hours. I would press ahead until routine was routine and not a hedge against memory. For many weeks I waged simultaneous war between love denied and the invasion of poetic battalions. I retraced our steps like a moon-struck school girl. The memory was made no more or less bitter. Later, it did become a warm memory. A willowy mantle of amendment—layers woven into a tapestry strong enough from which to hang a lifetime of layers—every thread needed for its mission.

My mind's eye thrives on an image of a miraculously delivered man. I have shared a few days and many letters with that man. Our meetings, mailings, and kinship renewed my determination to not settle for less than Charles. The windows of my heart I left open to admit all weathers blowing by from the humanity within my circumference. My heart tested breezes for a scent of attachment. I would have welcomed another such meeting of minds. Another man. I did not spurn options. There simply was no other who appeared with the force of recognition I felt for Charles or who appeared before the door of marriage was bolted. My natural affections disappeared into heart-crippled darkness after I was forced into a betrothal without swoon, into a bridal act without ceremony, and enshrouded by shards of crushing distrust. In a day—with many unhappy returns.

Austin never seemed to think himself miraculously connected. He expected a friendly, functional wife who would respond to his maintenance and charity. He got cold ambition. A bitter, hollow dose. Austin spent more and more time in our old home, away from the shrillness of Sue. We talked. His palpable unhappiness was eased by my company. Vinnie and I studied his comfort—much like the days of childhood. I read poems to him. He approved. I wrote more. He was my male companion, a conversational lifeline in the absence of Charles.

Having known Charles endures as a blessing. I wear it like a robe that presses warmly against every part of my being. It stretches over me in-home or yard. It bars the path to melancholy. It keeps me tied to the little line of tasks in my daily lot.

March 23, 2008

MY KINDRED SPIRIT WAS NEARBY. I STAYED AWAY. NEARNESS evoked an abiding template of a wish—for someone—educated, articulate, with a similar cultural background. Best of all, a comrade in liminality.

> my tongue caught
> mangled and frayed
> like floss
> can't work as it should
> now that you're here

Time around him was in groups—busy talkative assortments. I enjoyed rich language from a distance. To be fair though, distance was the hallmark of all my interactions with people. Distance guarded my core badness. I was still some years away from leaving behind my pervasive sense of being flawed. Being divorced did not help. Single women of my generation were often cast in the role of poacher. Having left my husband, my interest in annexing someone else's was presumed. Wives did not exactly draw aside their skirts in my presence but their suspicion was evident. My ever-vigilant brain always picked up those signals.

I raged at the history that consigned me to isolation. Rage itself accomplished nothing. But when I was able to look squarely at sections of my history—at childhood, my teen years, at young womanhood—none experienced consciously, an enormous sadness ensued. Sadness accomplishes a lot. Tears restore balance, even by way of eyes swollen to slits from crying.

Distance worked. I feared the turbulence of yearning. Distance failed occasionally. I was blind-sided one spring day years ago when my daughter and I waited in a ticket line for a community event. As we waited, he exited nearby. Salutations were exchanged. I mimicked his accent badly. He aarrghed with glottal vigor, turned his head slightly so that I saw a one-eyed twinkle and half a smile. The heart-tweaking kinship flashed. I had enough experience at that point to know that tweaking was beyond my control. But for a second I felt at home.

I dreaded that robbed of breath feeling followed by hours of letdown. Of resuming my not-so-exciting everyday life. Part of the letdown was the inevitable eruption of my 'bad' self who had no problem reminding me of all my flaws. It helped when I called to mind the qualities of this person that might be troublesome. Like organization and time challenges and perhaps the trendy scourge of depression. My brain easily turned those into deal-breakers—negative self-talk on behalf of both of us that deflected longing.

> I have worn a track
> by endless returns
> to a shrine
> of hope
> for a kindred spirit
> who would seize me
> with gratitude
> after many supplications
> at a shrine of his own

I remember myself as a young woman. Slender, nice legs, relatively fit, fashionably clothed. Generally acceptable. Although my round, doughy face was framed by baby fine and thin hair, eyelashes, and brows. All unstylish and unchanged for decades. My short jawline made for a thick neck. All was plain, verging on homely.

Internally, I had done real work. Counseling had given me a name for this part of my circumference and a process for reframing. It let me consider triggers and new perceptions. At the same time, my public persona and what lived behind it needed time, an unspecified amount, to move closer together on the healing continuum. The process of rebuilding my core self as someone with value and separateness had all the fragility of a newborn. This hesitant self was painfully slow in redefining my connection to the world, in letting me believe in myself as a 'catch' if not a 'babe.'

My Divine connections were solid. The failure of human agency kept me turned toward the other world. A world that sent 'knowings' in the form of new consciousness. I availed myself of all that my hyper-vigilance screens deigned to admit. Though I tried to monitor books, conversations, and dreams to keep it slant, as Emily would say.

Dreams were and are frequent visitors entering with flagrant disregard for my careful efforts at image control. Their shimmer left shifting veils that tantalized with scenes of panic alternating with reassurance. With some frequency, my sleep was split by lethargic big, black snakes flaccidly lying around emoting threat. Deadweight waiting to be transmuted. These dreams were not like Emily's pink, lank and warm worm that became a snake with mottles rare when she tried to tie it to the bedpost. Her dreams were pre-Freud, so she was not burdened with reductionist phallic symbolism. In her dream, fright sent her fleeing down a long road to a different town.

In most cultures snakes represent transformation. A continual shedding of old, ill-fitting, itchy skin for a new external that functions until it too splits under the pressure of growth that can not be stifled. I see our snakes as a spiral string between new and old knowings. They mediate wisdom that can be teased out to make life easier. Wisdom that can balance ego urges with a broader sense of purpose or call. The more I am willing to consider the suggestions implicit in dreams, books, and conversations, the more reliably knowings arrive with modest but deepening levels of initiative and self-care.

Like Emily, I wish that people who emote, who claim and voice experiences of Otherness, were not so few and far between. In the end, I am grateful for jolts of kinship. Recently, I had the occasion to walk through a large room. I felt a sweet, heart-tugging instant of warm content. As I continued to walk, I realized that I had unknowingly passed within feet of this man. What a lovely gift from the universe. From my kin in the collective unconscious.

March 28, 2008

A SEED'S ENCODED URGE TO SPROUT WILL DO SO, WHEN MINIMAL
requirements for light and water are met. In varied environments
and times, gardens grow. We live because there are gardens.
The outdoors is fearful yet fascinating. Maybe the fearful part
is that we know weather patterns can eliminate landscapes or
species. And as humans, we claim to manage our existence. Yet
the fascinating complexity of gardens, forests, and prairies do
not let us forget that we choose between that management and a
willingness to accommodate nature's boundaries.

When I feel powerless, not managing well, I mingle with
residents of a nature that have life energy and cellular structure,
but no consciousness. It is a relief to walk on the paths of their
endurance for a while. Among trees or along waterfronts, I am
returned to a rustic state of harmony. This harmony was common
among dwellers of past generations who had to be minutely in
tune with their surroundings to survive.

Now instead of keeping a keen eye on the clouds, wind, rain,
or the local volcano, we watch an inner landscape. Depression,
addiction, behavioral and attention issues, productivity, and
wealth occupy brain space. This inner frontier leads to the edge of
consciousness. After that . . . What? the Unknown, the Void, the
Mystery, the Great Spirit, the whatever, a higher power?

Emily was an avid gardener. Natural images and creatures
inhabit the dips and rises of her poems. I believe she understood
gardens to be external and internal—. . . *Here* is a little forest /

Whose leaf is evergreen; / Here is a brighter garden, / Where not a frost has been; / In its unfading flowers . . . / Into *my* garden come!

Emily did not try to suppress nature's effect. Her interior garden of ideas and feelings burned with frost and sun. A garden of fearless reflection. As necessary and sustaining to her as the vegetable plots in her backyard.

Em, you were closer to rural, natural life. The fact that you had less to occupy your eyes does not diminish nature's role in your world. You trusted the growth and renewal in nature. The nodding ascent of flowers in a fury of bloom.

> insight surfaces
> in unblemished beginnings
> with the relief of clarity
>
> insight hardens
> thoroughly in place
> a dried complacency
>
> insight yields
> to brittle husks
> sureness ruined
>
> insight hides
> in drifted dens
> change nurtured

You lived close to natural rhythms without our modern urge to twist it to your own ends. Humility in the face of natural limitations is not a hallmark of this century's culture.

September 15, 1885

Fall is a full-feeling time. Mounds of cold sand in the cellar cover roots destined to be chunks in our winter soup. Our cellar shelved gem-like rows of bottled jams, fruits, and vegetables given by summer to keep us alive in the long dark. Fortunate we are too, for the means to purchase tea, coffee, sugar, and flour. With these comestibles, we will saturate our inside circumference with the scent of stew, soup, bread, and pie.

Today, I spent a sunny morning in my garden off the dining room. Cheer, unannounced, may call when I'm in a garden. Its calling card revives my alliance with all creaturely comrades. Such a utilitarian spot holds shoots of green and me, both with our small strivings to stay on terra firma, to turn our sturdy appendages toward light.

In my fall garden, shells of summer selves degrade into soil without resistance. Garden beds have dirt covers pulled over their roots that are left to rot into readiness for the next generation. Tools are oiled and stored. Shriveled stalks and furrows are exposed, waiting for snow to soften and even their edges. My reliance on my garden off the dining room will be pressed into greater service when winter replaces the warm mercies of summer. I will play a spring trick on sweet bulbs and use light and sun to force them into yielding early blossoms.

The delight of plants for my eyes and my heart is not their sole appeal. It is the revival they represent, the reassurance of life repeating year in and year out. Flora does not know that they repeat. They simply follow instructions from roots or seeds. Roots that can apparently see in the dark or feel a few degrees of rising temperature. When icy dirt melts, plants send up stems.

That I can take this tenacity off the shelf and hold it to my bosom in the drear of grey days is a gush of summer light. The support it offers, I embrace. I thank them with whispers from upwellings of feeling and the caress of my fingers.

The sun takes its turn to pull up a cover of shadow—to rest—weary of lighting my way—the light we share fades into a memory of day. I am consoled to know that sun will slip like breath back into tomorrow. How satisfying to find myself still in this marvel.

March 31, 2008

MY IDEA OF A GARDEN LIVES IN MY HEAD, APART FROM THE FIVE big pots on my balcony impersonating a garden. The plants are colorful. They screen my view of flat, gravel-covered garage roofs so my eye can merge balcony greenery with that of the treetops beyond. Just three of the containers really count, because the Norfolk Pine and the Yucca are houseplants that will be granted floor space as soon as the killing effects of frost come to town. Houseplants clearly are not the same as my memory of dark ridges running across the yard.

The garden in my head was a real garden. One that my dad tended in our backyard when I was young. Toward the end of May, the proud possessor of the neighborhood rototiller would turn last year's dregs into this year's fertile platform. He set out rows, planting legumes in a different place each year so that the nitrogen in their roots fed sprouts. He impaled a wooden stake at one end of a row and unfurled the attached twine until another stake was stuck in at the other end. Straight, even rows were the result, with little mounds for marrows in their own corner.

This turning and hoeing of furrows inevitably exposed fat, dirt-flecked, oily-looking earthworms that squirmed in my dad's hand. He would ask, "Want to hold one?" "Uh, no, no thanks." Looking was the limit of my curiosity. All summer I tromped between the rows with nary a thought to the contribution of crawlers below. I yanked carrots from wormy dirt and ate them with just a quick wipe to remove the larger clods. I looked for overripe peas left too long on the vine, ones that escaped picking for the tender, lightly boiled, popping with flavor peas we ate for lunch. I would eat each large mealy green pea separately. And I never ate the pods, though now the sugar snap peas from the store go down pod and pea together.

My contribution apart from avoiding earthworms was picking raspberries. Once they fruited, I was required to pick every day. A challenging task as bees zoomed around the little white blossoms tucked among prickly edged leaves and thorny stalks. The raspberries were huge. I wore them on my fingers like thick wooly hats before sucking them into my mouth and pressing them between the roof of my mouth and my tongue until a red river of juice ran around my teeth. Once in a while when I buy raspberries, I get a pint that tastes like berries right off the canes. The taste transports me back to the garden, the bees, my sunhat, and my bowl. My mother still makes raspberry jams and jellies with purchased fruit instead of the backyard variety. At least not her backyard.

One day I was reading a book about Emily and was amazed to discover her description of a garden in her brain. Each of us, independently, a hundred years apart, knew and used gardens as an archetype for the eternal, for the cycle of beginnings and endings. In her writing, she used the reality of gardens, insects, and birds as symbols to represent love, success, yearning, duty, and death. She tended her inner plot, as I do, carefully letting insight and gratitude blossom.

A little musing on any of those subjects shows that growing plants is similar to growing a self. Gardens, whatever their scale, are alive. They required tending. If we neglect them, they wither or retreat into dormancy if not actual death. Untended people— marginalized by insufficient education or health care, poverty— the numbing effects of materialism or just endless superficial encounters may wither as well and bear no fruit.

September 20, 1885

AFTER THE SHEEN OF SPRING PASSED AND PLANTS RACED TO
reach light, blossom, or set fruit in their allotted span, a little of
their soft energetic striving slipped up stems and fastened onto
my fingers. Kneeling on my red blanket with my hands near soil
and leaves, the sun and water coursing through their tiny tubes
left my heart swelling in reply. I steady myself with stillness
and slow breathing to distill the moment, sure that any small
movement would dissolve my reverie. If a youthful Austin had
been nearby, laughter and a spoiler's remark about swollenness of
the lower regions would have been lobbed into our conversation.
No sabotage intended . . . nevertheless . . . gentlemen and their
preoccupations.

Heart swelling finds me among sprouts, rhizomes, or
runners emerging according to plan. Do we not try the same? Do
we not find ourselves reaching for light, following it throughout
the day, and waiting for its return? In my hurry or my leisure,
there are moments when my heart does swell. My soul stirs. The
universe has said hello.

From the garden rows, an occasional bit of flamboyant
red flashed from shadow. Flaunting really, a spurt of cardinal
feathered, like heart's blood streaking across summer green.
Such a flicker of life force caused quite a stir, a swelling. That
stirring—soul-stirring—grew from my garden work until
it became habitual. I discovered that not even quiet was
required. Just a pause to notice. Creeping green tendrils cause

heart-stirring—cause anger to dissolve into tears. I call on stirrings for comfort. They became allies.

I am content to find the cheerful proclamation of bird and flower and bee competing in harmony. Though if there are crows, they have to be first and loudest. Trilling and buzzing are drowned. A tree bronzed by late afternoon light holds a quiet-for-now crow. Distance makes it dull black, a smudge in a surround of alive golden leaves. The tranquil confines of my garden runs to rub shoulders with the life of wild fields and unkempt woods nearby.

April 5, 2008

UNSEASONABLY OPEN WINDOW WEATHER. EMILY, FROM MY ERA the same raucous, raspy, abrasive crows are still fighting or flirting. Who knows. If only they would do it later. Or learn how to inquire politely, "May we caw this early?" With my alarm clock, phones, bleeping timers, and electronics, I try to respect the earshot of others. This is not the gift of crows. I do credit them with the ability to split light with their dark shadows slashing through sky like flung black scythes. Flying things flock through the sky. Flinging sound around like atmospheric litter— be it wind-blown bird song or the monstrous roar that trails in the wake of unmelodic metal birds. I prefer little brown bird friends that have less intrusive early chirps and humbly disguise themselves among mutual curves of gray-brown branches.

Nature may surprise me into reflection if it can sneak past my sensory brakes. Brakes that are always applied to some degree lest rogue sunbeams, bird song, or a scented breeze challenge a calm moment. Brakes let me live a millimeter, a nanosecond, outside reality. Because even a sudden crow can trigger hyper-vigilance, one of the sorry hallmarks of post-traumatic stress. Unexpected loud sounds—arguing voices an aisle over at the store, playground screamers, revving motorcycles, sirens, a crying baby—can trigger the alertness, fast breathing, poor concentration, and muscle tension of an adrenaline rush. Exhaustion and backache are the leftovers from stress reactions that repeat and repeat.

My hair-trigger vigilance became maladaptive long ago. At least now I understand how it works. What used to keep me safe has to be asked to moderate its incursions, while I repattern my brain reactions with positive self-talk and biofeedback breathing so I stay in the moment. Mentally and physically.

September 30, 1885

LOOK AT A LEAF—ANY LEAF. PERHAPS ONE GREENING AS IT
curls from a cracked winter casing or a leaf that has been around,
knows all there is to know about its sphere on plant or tree, or a
leaf ready to be elsewhere, dry carbon shards pushed off by the
next generation forming behind. Any leaf. Compact little ovals
edged by their defense of small serrations, or spikey maples, or
the round convolutions of elms.

Any leaf and I am calmed. I hold a life-cycle, a natural span,
a journey whose staunch comfort never palls. My lungs slow.
My shoulders ease. Composure spreads and smooths out worry.
From seconds spent with a leaf, I am returned useful, indeed,
valued in my circumference.

In the seasons of all climes, thoughts of mortality mingle
amid the cycle of regeneration, growth, decay, and dormancy.
Some dormancy continues to death. All that is on earth for a
sojourn as a recognizable entity—an insect, an animal, all manner
of herbage, a human—returns the remnants of itself to reform in
continuing creation. My eternal spirit notwithstanding—a corner
of me cries not to molder in the dregs of decay. One of legions
become earth. The record of my words in tidily tied stacks set
orderly in a bottom drawer, will no doubt follow suit.

April 10, 2008

IN IMAGINATION, I SEE MY BLOOM-SPATTERED BALCONY. A SPRAY of color. My pots are a physical equivalent of going to 'a happy place.' I can sit on my third-floor perch in sun or wind or dark, screened from cars and neighbors on nearby balconies. My plants, in the guise of a garden, turn a concrete slab balcony into an outdoor nook that is as close to a yard as an apartment dweller gets.Other balconies are dotted with faded coolers, dusty barbecues, or other cast off bits and pieces as well as the occasional smoker leaning heavily on a railing.

This approximation of a garden is what I can have since thick chunky marrows could not thrive in such a confined space. Sitting in the company of living things, however small, encourages me. I am like a vine creeping over ridges in bricks or like a flower blooming from a muddy track, working hard to establish a tough but fragile base for more growth.

I am not directly connected to dirt apart from occasionally repotting a houseplant and vacuuming leaf litter. I do not have the daily, primal connection Emily had. A garden, inside or out, is not part of my survival mode. My bond is reduced to observing seasonal changes while I walk on groomed paths near woods and water.

Living alongside the life-and-death essence of the natural world can be intense. Emily lived in this proximity on a daily basis. The piquancy in her writing suggests this. Unslanted truth popped out of her consciousness, demanding recognition.

Closeness to the elements and a global sense of wellbeing from insight flying in full-blown means that mental materials have to be marathon-ready every moment.

Emily, you had no one at hand to share the mind-bending realities you wrote into poems. No one to validate the keenness of the knowings. Knowings you passed along through eye and ear-catching details for those with eyes and ears to see and hear. You pointed to details of mind and body—hills casting off their bonnets, mermaids in the basement, bobolink choristers, and wild nights.

Each of us can notice details that function as our own signposts toward claiming insight and wisdom. Emily, I am tempted to believe that claiming was easier in your smaller circumference with its slower pace, compared to my contending with a global village stuck in the play position that heaves information at me day and night. As tempting as it is to think insight inroads were easier for you, I rather think that each of us has our own measure of deafness that blocks the intrusive language of transformation and ascent to new levels of understanding.

I like to imagine you, Emily, threading down garden rows, rubbing petals on your cheek or fingers between the particular redolence of damp earth and the fragrant tickle of floral scent trails. All the while, your garden roots your mind in ideas about patience in dormancy and risk in trying again.

Your garden of cycles showed you life that moves. Showed you moments strung together—be they moments from memory, or the present moment, or a peek toward vague future moments. Moments are like Celtic knots that loop back and around, with no beginning and no end. Knots that keep history and future close in a spiral. Emily, thoughts about insight, cause me to wonder if your garden was an archetype for you. A symbolic form around which meaning coalesced. A reference point you returned to repeatedly. Hmm.

November 18, 1885

UPON REFLECTION—A LITTLE TRAVERSE ALONG TRACKS OF
reminiscence—the men with whom I had mental attachments
were professionals and much older than I. Yes, undeniably. As
compared to the good providers who head-lined the contenders
among my age mates. Reasonable enough, when species renewal
was needful.

In the male sector of my circumference I sought, I hoped
for, bold informed discourse among Austin and Father's friends.
That these men were married was of no consequence. I sought
the refreshment of verbal sparring. I think of this when I consider
Charles. My standard-bearer.

The idealization of Charles made my soul sleek and lively. It
gave me hope and patience amid my many daily labors. Would
the arrival of guests have been a welcome enrichment to daily
discussions with Charles? I can only imagine. The dream of wild
nights filled me for a time—woke me with wanting.

The days-to-years of distance did change me. Longing
left. Left me free to cherish all the rest that crept or popped into
my presence—day by day. Left me with layers of soul fat to fuel
moments of privation when they came. But then the litany of grief
so taxed my bodily economy that my sleek soul emaciated and
ceased function.

My 'Lord,' Judge Otis, was the last amiable promise
to leave me. Our long, filial acquaintance began to wander
intrepidly toward Eros after his wife's death. Truly, tenderness

has not a date . . . it comes and overwhelms . . . each incursion more Divine. This was not the devouring blaze of Charles, but smoldering embers that could be coaxed into brief but intense bursts of flame when gently breathed upon. I no longer had heart space for the idolatry of love that in years past created such anguish and elation.

Letters, my preference for communicating, were our lovely relief. My Lord and I had corresponded for years, friendly fisticuffs over matters of mutual interest. Our exchanges warmed. Each looking for light through a veil of loss. This was someone I could live with, not live through. That he selected me, invited me, was a delicious point of return amidst my churning sea of loss. Marriage was an unlikely consideration. Could I believe that he was not looking for a replacement chatelaine? And I could not easily leave the grooves worn in my home of many years. Our older ages were breeders of illness and one of us might well become a burden. In spite of our losses, or perhaps because of the losses, I tip-toed with delicacy toward the prospect of a new unknown. Just watch the spring in my step. My pen is full of words.

When I learned that heart attack had stolen him—I stood in yet a broader gulf of light snuffed by loss. Gulfs of recent residence collected themselves to create utter dark. Imagination was my only sight. I lay and watched the sun redistribute light. I could see the universe moving while I remain rooted to my spot, my chair, my feet to the floor. I must send the sun my choices— send the many points of my circumference that were or might have been otherwise—so my spirit can rest in light.

April 18, 2008

LOST LIGHT LIKE IDEALIZATIONS ABOUT LOVE AND
connection may need to be lost. My fragile value allowed me
only abstract thoughts about relationships. Through abstraction,
meek self-possession was preserved intact. I enjoyed life in the
rocking undulations of the middle minus heart-surges of hope
at one extreme and devilish cackling, 'who do you think you are'
at the other. My strategy was to focus on the routine of work,
writing, baking, and reading.

One summer, in my rediscovery process, I decided to diet.
I am not a diet sort of person, have never needed to, but slow
middle-aged metabolism, a worn-out thyroid, and my empty-nest
indulgence in happy food contrived to leave love handles capable
of hefting vast poundage.

> a winter of cookies
> to sweeten
> my sadness caught up to me
> and rolled right on over
> past rounds and squares
> bars and slices
> keeping my roundness
> around
> weighted with sweet and sad

The diet program promised to help me lose weight and
feel good through fewer calories and a flood of macro and
micronutrients. As soon as I began, my brain protested, "Oh, my

dear, you can not change your body without changing the mind and spirit that drives it . . . so, sweetie, we'll hold on to the pounds while your mind sheds a bundle of physic weight." And the brain had its way. It always does.

I felt like Gretel, grasping for guiding crumbs as I traced my way back. The path was more familiar for me than Gretel. I had been on it before, revisiting and tending to pieces of my past that needed to be reframed. This new lap through the process was triggered by the diet. I felt drawn to ideas of self-love and personal value. At such times, I rummaged through my bookcases looking for the words of friends. There was a quote that niggled just outside my awareness. A quote that had shot precisely through the ether once before. I found it. The Spanish philosopher, Ortega Y Gasset says that . . .

> we fall in love on few occasions in a long life. It is a rare and fortuitous event, and it strikes incredibly deeply. When such love happens, it is for no other reason than the singularity of the object. Only this person. Not attributes and virtues, not voice or hips or bank account, not projections left over from earlier flames or hand-me-down family patterns, simply the uniqueness of this person whom the heart's eye selected. Without that sense of fate in the choice, the romance of the love doesn't work.

I would quibble, and possibly excise projections and hand-me-down family patterns because I think they play a larger role than Ortega Y Gasset credits. But in the main, I believe that he is correct about the enchantment of spirit sparked by the long reach of unconscious kinship. The quote helped. I could see my own benchmark as an enchantment. Part of his spirit and mine must be very old friends. That those parts recognized each other—after forty years, three countries and two continents of separation— was not surprising. Apart from that, I was relieved to know that enchantment need not be romantic. Benchmark man was the right person at the right time to challenge an undeveloped track of my life. I began to view him as a composite, a talisman, who represented Providence, the vibe energy around each of us.

my feet are not
mired by mundanity
when I float
to a thin place
and find a home
unknown on earth

Considered further, I decided that I have 'fallen in love' four times in my life. Two of the four are women. It made even more sense that these kinship strikes may not be romantic but energies, grace perhaps, from my vibe frequency. They get my attention. They show me how connection feels. The first one is a soul sister whom I have known for many years. Second, is wedding man, who happened along before I had any skills for self-promotion or self-preservation. The third is benchmark man. And the fourth I did not get to know because when we met, she was an authority figure. Plus I admit that I avoided the unsettledness provoked by such encounters.

I held tight to the illusion that I could maintain control over what I let into my life. The forced entry of kindred spirit incursions raided my defenses. At the time, I simply did not recognize what was happening, did not have the ego strength to stop it. If my emotional development had been healthier, benchmark man would not have played such havoc in my consciousness. But quotes and a diet began to plug the gap in my boundaries with understanding and knowledge. Dare I say, even wisdom. Kindred spirits and my perspective can coexist.

As much as I had reframed and made operational adaptions over several years to reconnect with my circumference, the impact of the diet was more of an assault than PTS defenses could withstand. They crumbled over a weekend. I spent hours assembling quotes from books and typing them into tidy cheat sheets that steered me away from the caves of core badness. It was like unloading a gun that had been cocked for years. There was nothing left for it to defend.

The diet triggered weight loss, along with new understandings, and revised adaptions that paraded throughout my summer. Company and long conversations stopped making me tired. My usual speed in leaving social events slowed. Going home was the last thing I wanted. Core badness could be overridden. Transformed. I woke up each day feeling like it was a holiday. I was only a little miffed to realize that most people feel like that most of the time.

Scattered moments of well-being have been outliers in my existence. Before that summer they were drummed into the background by hyper-vigilance. During my diet summer, I basked in well-being that showed no sign of leaving. I considered tentatively the idea of friendship without dread or need. Alongside my history, tentative new value crept in. A visible, competent person emerged, wet-behind-the-ears, but not in need of external rescue. Little did I know how often how the cycle of recognition, acceptance, and letting go would repeat before becoming a new default.

> hope may be a thin place
> where existence makes sense
> I'd like more

January 15, 1886

I DREW COLUMNS, ORNAMENTED FOR THE IMAGINATION—
behind one is aligned the immolating ferocity of young love and
behind the other is the dignified glow of the companionable ashes
of experience. Each works in its own way.

I do not miss the intensity of attachment that occludes
judgment, social convention, and laws that bound behavior.
Jane Eyre calling for one's heart lives in fiction, not in the
pedantic considerations of home. Still, the appeal of Jane and
Mr. Rochester endures. Do we not hope for them while ignoring
complexity beyond consummation?

Do they not suggest that if we suffer and wait—the throat-
tightening, gait-slowing, mind-numbing, limb-immobilizing,
tongue-cleaving yearning—will be answered? Like a story
contained neatly between book covers. Like Pascal's God-shaped
space, we hurry to fill it with anything except divine energy
that waits with patience behind our digressions and material
provision.

Volcanic young love is taken timidly as reason for betrothal
with whatever suspecting or unsuspecting human object is at
hand. The heady time of courtship slips into housekeeping, work,
and family—each on its separate and divergent path. Yearning
thought to be satisfied may break through again. Some, like
Austin and Mabel, seek another, a human answer for their God-
shaped space. Others find that blood's fervor has cooled and
respond to stirrings by admitting their own incapacity. Sense

prevails and the line behind the second column lengthens. They are the ones who look for a different solution on the path of unsettledness. Good works litter that path. Many engage so firmly that they stand accused of overwork. Burying oneself in work is often a path for literally being buried. Father was one who trod that path.

What they miss, whether they choose human or occupational distraction, is the chance to sit with longing—to hold it—to trace it back to its Divine source and ask what it wants.

I sit down with my mine—and find seconds of suffusion in which I know the surety of abiding joy in the doing of ordinary tasks. I look forward to glimpses of small such glories and the attendant belonging that scattered across my hours. Consent to one's circumference appears to be a facet of this grace. When I stopped wanting a life of my sole devising, stopped envying the plans of others, stopped competing, then my environs revealed windows that gave onto novel unfolding mysteries. My forest grove church, my garden toil under glass or sky became manifestations of Divine presence. Discovery in the language of my own life.

Humans want control, not submission to the ancient and wise energy of the universe. After many upwellings of the Divine—it is no small agony for me to remember prim rote reciters at First Congregational—mimes doing as directed by the limitations of tradition and clergy. The tableau forms with good works in some evidence but seeking for the Jesus way is carefully kept outside the ivied walls of custom. My poetry is pressed into service to carry the weight of my words of longing for clarity, for peace. Others must attempt their own articulation.

April 30, 2008

FOR THOSE LIKE ME, WHO GIVE OUR SOURCES OF MEANING MORE
than a passing thought, one of my heroes is Marion Woodman,
a Jungian analyst who worked mostly with women's history
and women's issues. She wrote that a woman needs to find the
particular feminine archetype or reference point that helps make
life meaningful. A reference point functions as a hinge—it opens
to an image that reminds me of meaning. After I experience a
hinge moment life is different in a way I can articulate.

Several years before I read Woodman's book, I found my
archetype without knowing it. It is a woman in a painting—a
visual archetype. As it happens, paintings are picked fairly often
to represent archetypes. For her own archetype, Woodman claims
the Da Vinci Cartoon for St. Anne.

> Anne your hand
> a compelling sketch
> of charcoal curves
> benediction
> on a background
> pebbly with bits
> speckled strands locked
> into a textured mass of fiber
> colored ocher

on clay shades of earth
your hand hovers
over Mary
and absent Elizabeth
and their boys
cousins at play
with prescience

Similarly, Mark Doty has his lemons and oysters. A painting that he says makes feeling glow with light and transparency. Patricia Hampl has a girl before an aquarium. She described her as a modern woman looking at the world who reminded her of feminism and freedom. I joined this group with my painting called *The Song of the Lark* by Jules Breton.

I first saw the painting in 1972 at the Art Institute in Chicago. I bought a postcard of it. A few years later I found a bigger copy that I taped to a wall. After another few years, I found a poster. I liked the size but am still distressed over the poor color in the reproduction. That version I stuck in a plastic poster frame. I can go into my bedroom and look at it anytime, thirty-five years later.

When one of my daughters moved to Chicago a couple of years ago, I could hardly wait to visit her and my painting. A convenient bench colluded in my long, captivating study. I took a picture of it. While the photo colors are vivid, the details are less distinct than in the other representations. This in no way weakens its work on me from its spot on a wall. Once identified, few considerations seem able to diminish the impact of an archetype bestowed by a hinge moment.

The Song of the Lark was painted in England in 1884. The subject is a sturdy young peasant woman. She has broad, bare, and tanned hands and feet. Her feet are in the dirt of the bottom two-thirds of the painting. Skin, clothes, and dirt share every hue and tone of brown created. Her right-hand holds a gray-brown, curved scythe.

She is wearing a coarse, dun-colored skirt, with a lighter chemise and scarf tied babushka-style around her head. In the distance are dim, dreary farm buildings edged by scrubby trees that creep greenly into the scene. The sky is a dazzle of gold tangerine sunset.

My girl has paused, her body alert, her mouth dropped open attentively as she listens at the end of a toilsome day to the larks, painted as distant black flecks on the sky.

When I look at this painting, I see a young woman living in an unlovely environment, who works hard physically but gives herself a moment to be lifted by sound and color. My brain lit up when it recognized another young woman quietly finding something that moved her in the midst of what seems like nothing.

A nothing that is the sameness of the daily round. But I am reminded, when I look at her, to name that which gives me pause. I am prodded to examine my current rut, to feel grateful, and to feel my connection to the eternal feminine.

I read Woodman's book, *Addiction to Perfection*, in 1982. When I got to the section about a feminine archetype, I knew that *The Song of the Lark* functioned for me as an archetype or reference point. When I look at my painting—it does not feel like idolatry—it feels like the Divine talking to me in my language. How else would I understand? Or experience a sense of connection? Reference points function like a trellis from which wobbly tendrils of self-possession cling. New tendrils let art or sound stand in for all the places where religion, politics or community let me down. My own self-possession grows stronger in proportion to decreasing dependence on external tribal norms. The numinosity of this painting lasts. It challenges me to think about what is seen and unseen.

If you are interested in a hinge moment bump from an archetype of your own—the first step is discovery. Don't look too hard. Wonder, to begin with—and ask—'what might a reference point be for me?'—and wait. It may be an image that is already nearby and pops into mind when you simply ask the question. It must pop into mind with an 'ah-hah.' The ah-hah is important. It can be had in a crowd, or alone, outside, inside, reading, talking, or connecting with a memory—but if the potential archetype is not accompanied by breath-catching or a halt of some degree, then pleasure is present but not a reference point. Once found, it stays, and you can tap its figurative salve anytime to let the truth of its neural energy work on you.

For Emily, her connection to nature anchored the floating sensation that is an insidious feature of solitude. She expressed her solidarity with eternal feminine archetypes through words and the outdoors. She established her course in the face of considerable opposition. Her father had her 'vetted' by a minister at First Congregational to satisfy himself that she was not on a short path to heresy or hell. The minister, to his credit, issued a verdict of soundness.

Emily lived a resolute nonconformity——her aesthetic sense and her survival skills honed by standing attendance to her home and garden tenants. The re-orienting effect of her nature archetypes kept her in the vicinity of Goodness. It was a respite of abiding Goodness beyond all contrived cultural convention.

March 30, 1886

IF ETERNAL TRUTH FLOATS AROUND US LIKE CLOUDS THEN THE same thoughts and perceptions repeat and repeat. Though at intervals it seems—someone has eyes to see—ears to hear and eases a cloud of unknowing into knowing for their circumference.

Do people have to experience knowing themselves? Is some knowledge too deep for words that it can not be given to us through another's experience? Is that why there are many creedal people and few who tread beyond the tone-deaf flatness of their tribe and creed? I fled the creedal decrees of First Congregational—I was confined by Father on earth but I refused to believe that Divine Being would confine me in any respect—in all matters the infinite stays with me where I am—using the existing elements of my circumference to assuage worry and confusion. To ready my ground for gifts.

Early, I felt as if I had a root running right through my center. A sturdy root full of sustenance not just perennial but eternal. I was born with this core—my job—to keep it in trim. I felt the roundness of time and gradually encroaching revelation.

I lived into it by the drop of each day. Each day added polish—perhaps the modest polish of a plain day of occupations succeeding each other in satisfying order—or   the high polish of a day of gladness.

I have a small recollection of being sent away to stay with a Norcross aunt, mother's sister when Vinnie was born. I had no say in where my small body was taken. Even then I had a watchful eye on my essence that had to stand sentinel stalwartly against invasions of influence from beyond my circumference. My notion of circumference germinated at a tender age. I knew the difference between my reliable center and the shifting sands on which I had to conduct myself.

My core was invaded finally by what the doctor called "revenge of the nerves." Who but death had wronged them? My breaths became tiny, so as not to cause riot in the air around me. The tight view from my eyes became blurred and words an ululating slur. My bones unjoined. Thoughts refused to cohere. I felt strongly dependent on the support of routine. Tasks I normally avoided, with small apology, became invested with life-giving agency. They absorbed all my concentration, functioned like stepping stones, showing me where to put my feet, how to occupy my hands.

Into those weeks of moments, when my mental process was detached, each day seemed endless. Yet months taken as a whole sped by in their emptiness.

Reprieves from weeks in that dim country were few. A welcome cleft in the armor of despair was my custom of sitting with my friends from a nearby universe. They warmed me—then bade farewell until I could stay with them and tarry for an eon or two in a love so lavish as to obviate any other need.

May 5, 2008

A LOVE SO LAVISH—HOW LONG CAN I HOPE? W. B. YEATS SAYS
that too long a sacrifice can make a stone of the heart. I've given
up waiting. In all of my life's stages, I believed myself to be
fatally flawed—physically, mentally, and spiritually—never good
enough. This was countered only by an inherent instinct that had
claws as deeply gouged in my psyche and spat out the message
that I could be enough if I tried and tried and waited and waited
. . . and I did . . . semi-consciously through childhood, my teens,
my college years, my marriage and early motherhood. I waited on
circumstances to change or on people or on knowledge to arrive.
In a half-life fog, I waited for externals to save me.

There was waiting within waiting, for the alarm clock, for
payday, for the next improving book, the next escapist book, for
birthdays, for seasons, all filled with potential for a difference
in how I lived. I began to hate the word "wait." It stuck to me
like a quiescent burr that might send up puncturing shoots of
restlessness or tension in any given moment.

With the eyes of hindsight, I can see waiting as a progressive
incubation that piled up. My intellect told me that there is no
time but the moment I am in. That I will never go anywhere that
is more important than where I am. In small ways, I learned to
honor myself. A parade of treats passed by, such as bubble baths,
new shoes, new recipes, a bit of decorating, clean laundry, or a walk
amid whatever elements weathered the day. Still, these newfound

enjoyments were mostly solitary. I altered my view of myself but could not imagine that anyone else could regard me favorably.

My sense of waiting has not disappeared but I admit it as a friend who needs attention. It's like a pearl drop of water poised in perfect tension on the tip of a pointed leaf. It waits suspended over an abyss. Water drops are not self-aware or waiting to drop would scare them witless. In their own wholeness, they fall, land and splinter. A drop might add molecules to an existing body of water or it might hit a hard surface with a scratch of erosion or sink into porous earth to sustain other life forms.

I am a drop. One that waited and waited to feel worthy. To fall and reform each day into value that fills and spills over again and again.

Trust, trust in the moment, focus on myself, let go of outcome and sink into palpable spaciousness . . .

> meaning is an agreeable guest
> welcome night or day
> it makes unexpected stops
> but will not stay
> lest I lie overlong
> in its fleeting bed

April 4, 1886

I WONDER IF I WAS INTENDED TO DIE YOUNG. MANY DAYS I WAS ready—death do kindly stop for me! Your slow carriage toward eternity needs only me in gown and tippet. Left behind is a life of many hurts. A hard life in soft creaturely conditions—and no one, in particular, will miss me. I have conquered no hearts, or minds for that matter. I am finished walking barefoot over the jagged terrain of my mind. Wishing for a companion who would bring shoes. Am I to be grateful for this?

I wonder if I have helped one fainting robin into her nest again? If I did, it happened outside my awareness. Possibly small favors—little kindnesses that seem so ordinary as to be stale is all our sweet Mystery requires. To the reality of the Divine, it may be sufficient to keep the orbiting sphere of humanity humming. My hundreds of letters were meant to be kind and thoughtful missives. Many returned the favor to me. As I am unwilling to receive company, news of the world will do.

Friendly details surround—my beloved slants of light, the many moods of my garden, the friendly slide of my pen, words capturing a semblance of the currents in my circumference. Such details pushed me through my days with little active arrangement on my part. Details that amassed into the shape of seclusion—that encroached into my quiet corner while my mind grew as the stage for performance of ideas bombinating around in my head. After arriving as intellectual tickles, knowings twisted their way through my heart to my pen—every word had a place—every page enough for the words it pillowed. Words out and inscribed—left space to be filled with new ones. Truly we turn not older with years, but newer every day.

May 12, 2008

a bone china jug
formed leafy and floral
by fingers feeling curves
and eyes shaping grace

a blow begins a web
for life-giving liquid
to flow from cracks

loss alters the grace
of my shape leaving behind
a tainted vessel that taunts
wholeness

May 15, 2008

EMILY, I HAVE OFTEN CALLED TO MIND THE COMMENT YOU dropped into my awareness years ago. The day you 'said' you did not want this to happen to anyone else. What was or is the "this" that you didn't want to happen? Perhaps at day's end with ordinary function safely on autopilot, my brain was less defended against extraordinary function. In that state, I shuffled to find comfort between heat and a service job that brought daily small death to much synaptic coherence. Were you a version of Rilke's future living in me long before it actually happens? Did you wait specifically for me for more than a hundred years after your physical departure?

A common understanding in physics suggests that a hundred years is a blink in the time dimension of the universe. I accept the premise of other dimensions. I accept them in the same way I accept microwaves I cannot see but like hot soup. In the way that I listen to music, but cannot see sound waves.

It seems that some who have passed from one dimension to another remain close to the world they left behind—in galactic pigeon holes for guides. Are these kindred spirit guides yoked to those yet to be? What a fantastic thought. If it is so, they are part of my real-time kinship circles. And I can meet kindred spirit remnants anytime as they nudge through Eliot's choir invisible. Muses.

After our previous pages of chat, we do have similarities. We both chronicled image and impression bubbling up from gray brain convolutions. Each of us had a kinship experience that set a standard for relationships, albeit through heartache. For different reasons, we spent a lot of time alone—exiles of a sort.

We both believed ourselves to be outside the conventions of our era. Outside internal and external conventions. The external certainty of your Victorian era began to crumble under the onslaught of Edwardian science and industry. New thoughts were abroad. Freud and psychoanalysis were invading. Your life was a bend in the road behind these emerging realities. A generation before women's rights had permanent prominence. Yet your poetry contains the whole palette of awakening, accepting, and adapting to what is. Testimony, in truth, for a common and eternal journey of the mind in every age. A universality that rioted in ranks of color from the garden in your brain. Increasing consciousness was the experience behind the words. A thoughtful experience that you claimed rather than the mind-numbing revivalism flooding your New England nook.

My mild unconventionality barely registers in an era where the sacred and the private are paraded around like severed heads on spikes. Allowances are made and even encouraged for individual expression wherever it falls on the ever-extending continuum for thought and behavior. But still, few think beyond the enculturation of their origins. Thinking may lead to change. Change follows thinking that reaches a tipping point. It can take years. There has been more change in the external and internal conventions in my lifetime than in the lifetimes that separate us.

Media and materiality are the telltale marks for my era. Old touchstones that created community comfort are trampled in favor of me and my immediacy. The wake of this disregard leaves people likely to succumb to the loudest voices and unwilling to assume personal responsibility for much of anything. One frayed thread from the trampling is a revisionist attempt to revisit sacred texts. Texts written and sufficient for long-dead brown men in the Middle East. The vision of compassion and cooperation at the core of Abrahamic faiths has not changed, but it is reasonable to need new access.

I want spirituality—ensoulment—unravaged by patriarchy whose power stifles. That sullies compromise and tolerance. That favors ego over discernment. I want girls to remember only a time when language included them, when their own version of experience and participation mattered. I believe this will happen. Not soon. Emily, you had no such point of vantage. Nothing in your circumference augured for the prospect of change. Consciousness was not perceived to be evolving. Those few, including yourself, who absented themselves from the mid-1800s cultural party lines were written off when persuasion proved ineffective.

Then and now, you and I were left to form our own mechanisms for meaning outside of established tradition. But your pronouncement to me—I've kept circling back to it. I decided to read your poems again. Also, I had an opportunity for conversation with another Emily devotee. As we talked and as I read—scales fell from my eyes. How did I not know or understand sooner? I have always felt the anguish, the desolation, the menace in much of your writing. Your preoccupation with dying, with prison, with horror is abundantly clear. What ripped the scales off for me was the fusion of exploding images associated with trauma. My own history of trauma, though different, fell into consonance with yours.

You told us yourself. Two of your poems punched through when my slow on the uptake brain collided with a moment of kairos. You wrote . . . "What fortitude the Soul contains / That it can so endure / The accent of a coming Foot / The Opening of a door . . ." And "I would murmur if at last / The ones I loved below/ Permission have to understand/ For what I shunned them so—/ Divulging it would rest my Heart/ But it would ravage theirs—. . ."

I fell alarmingly far into the full numbness of a ravaged heart. Those words among a multitude of others became for me like Hansel scattering neon bread crumbs the size of boulders. I felt as if one of them smashed my solar plexus and left me gasping with the realization of what I now believe the 'this' was for you, the trauma you did not want to happen to anyone else. Your father's unholy incursion.

It took weeks for my self-admonishment to ease. I was part of the problem for so long. I, who thought I had eyes to see. Part of those weeks was a breast-beating grief for centuries of damage done to women. But enough time has passed for me to have talked myself away from that cliff edge. I acknowledge the path you created to preserve your identity—while perhaps protecting Vinnie—and perhaps protecting your wider community as well.

You gave me an indelible imprint with your comment and vanished except for the doors and windows of your poetry. As your energy edges around the margins of the earthly, I hope you feel the strength of your images that became nests of refuge and flight for flocks of us robins. If readers experience feeling from your words, if we find our public faces strengthened by private understanding—if insight becomes action, then writer mission accomplished.

Writing helped each of us balance the tension between self and tribe even while our pages initially languished in quiet, dark drawers. But our differences and similarities aside, we scream at the world to think—to vision—to foster initiative—to build word bridges with many lanes to travel between eroded old norms and nascent buds of common good growing through cracks in our collective psyche. All eras need to develop era-specific structures that transfer meaning. Your example has hurried me along—to press my hard-won private learnings into service for public reality—to stay close to the mystery of living a divine and human life—to add my harmony to my section of the choir invisible.

April 12, 1886

EACH MORNING ARRIVES TO LAY A THIN CORDIALITY OVER ME. Sustenance before rising. All in all, I would rather have new mornings than not. My eyes open in anticipation of freshness. My sense of urgent memories has slowed, but my curious search for new ones has not! I say curious because, in spite of illness, a day is an amazement of breath and flash of pleasure offered in and out of season.

By noontime's tall sun, the day has settled, perhaps into sameness, nothing much beyond my peeks into the tiny infinities turning all around me. Civilizations march on, in trees or beehives or anthills or flowers or neighboring homes for humans. Each a cradle, a haven, and a grave. Though I never gave birth to a child—I carried new life that made its presence felt, made a painful entry, and stayed to grow in influence over my endeavors.

As evening begins, dreams of hearth and the comfort of food pierce my aching nausea. Light starts sneaking away. I see soft indigo flowing outside. Did I accomplish anything today? I breathed. Invisibility invaded my nose and kept me here. I did write today. A few more loose threads clipped and tidied away.

I am ready to be called back. Darling Infinite has left me to loiter at Heaven's door. At day's end, I will crawl farther under the covers and hibernate for a while. Escape into a foretaste of other awayness.

I wonder if I will know the day of my summons? Will that dawn tell me to savor it particularly? Will it whisper through a midday sun warming me? Or maybe later I will simply sneak more deeply into evening shadow? Perhaps during sleep I will go. There will be a glad following when the kindness of death stops for me.

Who will bring first greetings? Charles, companion of my heart and Gilbert, blithe and elfin? Maybe my mother, a transformed mother, ready to reach for me, enfold me. Surely, Ben and Otis . . . all who have had a share in my existence. My heart will tighten when the universe beckons—others will set me orderly for burial—but I will have flown.

May 20, 2008

FOUR IN MY ACQUAINTANCE WERE DIAGNOSED RECENTLY WITH cancer. One terminal, two medium, and one mild. Two are younger than I. Do I consider my own death? Not often. I cherish an idea, an illusion some would say, that I am friends with my mortality. Not only will I go in peace, but will know the time and be filled with anticipation of a great reunion with my section of the choir invisible. But my response to death can only be abstract when its harbingers are not pointing directly at me.

A negative diagnosis is a bit like pregnancy. It may include illness, tiredness, and concern about the actual transition of birth or death. In the preparation for either, there are natural adjustments. There is plenty of advice. But the actual event is accomplished by the person making the transition. Granting free access to all the resources in your body for nine months is enough time to prepare for a new being. To be ready, to let go of a childless life. To have another person around permanently, body and spirit.

When a person is dying—some want to take care of unfinished business, take stock, check if there are regrets to amend, or perhaps fulfill last wishes. When illness has free access to all your resources, there may be less time to prepare. To let go of unrelenting pain and morphine-fogged consciousness. To be the body whose spirit goes—permanently.

New life enters the world quickly. With that first breath, a newborn turns from greyish-blue to pink in seconds. A life retreating leaves slowly, turning from pink to pallor over hours. This immense transition needs time. As if a spirit needs to practice severing its long connection to a body. I have been told that it is important to sit with the recently deceased for a period of time, maybe an hour or two to ensure that the spark—the animating energy—completes its transition.

Sudden death varies the process slightly. Opportunities abound for death-dealing trauma through our attachment to war, guns, substance abuse, and environmental degradation. The agitated energy of sudden disconnection suggests that our omnipresent vibe family helps the transition whether it is a slow easing or a rapid dive. In spite of a human penchant for creating hurt and misfortune, I believe that the vibe frequency of compassion is constant and dominant in the physical universe. Proximity is unrelated to our lifestyle choices.

In string theory, strings of similar energy vibrate on the same frequency. The strings of love and all goodness, all positives have a high, quick, and brilliant vibrancy. A quarky string dance deep in the realm of the Divine down in the universe of atoms.

Negatives have the energy of darkness, of bad intention, a dull, slow, vibrancy weighted by density. The thick energy of even tiny darknesses driven by ego, like unkind thoughts, mean or selfish words, drag me down from light dancing. The down may be brief. Into those moments of tiny hubris comes forgetfulness, confusion, cut fingers, stubbed toes, all sorts of bruises—from not quite missing the door jamb or the bed frame or the car roof.

I think it's likely that each moment or day in dark must be redeemed by an equal and opposite acquaintance with light. People whose emotional and spiritual development has been ruptured by addiction or abuse, reclaim their life from the moment the damage began. The healing and elevation of light flies over dark, even when it has to do so time and again. Recovery is faster, more thorough, each time. Each moment is like being in a bubble, an aura perhaps of honesty, generosity, and care as pure as can be. Waywardness in any portion weakens the

encasement of the bubble. And so I have learned to set a watch on
my thoughts, actions, and words.

I like the energy of light. I like belonging to a vibe family
of light. This is my circumference no matter how many sorry
returns I make in and out of small negatives.

In my immediate family, I have met one death. My dad
was diagnosed with idiopathic pulmonary fibrosis. Even though
he and my mother lived very expensive plane tickets away, the
granddaughters and I visited during his last three summers that
included his 90th and 91st birthdays.

After diagnosis, Dad's oxygen needs increased slowly
during his last couple of years. Exertion robbed him of breath. It
was difficult for him to dress or shave. He sat a lot. One Friday
night he fell. Tripped over his oxygen tube. He could not get up.
Paramedics came and helped, but he said that his back hurt. He
wanted to go to the hospital. He felt safe there, care was at hand,
and he did not worry about burdening or frightening my mother.

He seemed to know and accept that this was his time. He
was not able to eat much or talk: it just made him cough. Then
the scary shortness of breath was apparent. Monday he slept most
of the day. Letting go was visible. His skin became translucent
and lay flatter against his bones. He was pensively elsewhere.

My mom dozed in a bed next to her companion of fifty-
seven years. Close enough to hold his hand. She sat up about
midnight on Monday, roused by loud music.

My dad was sleeping. She checked the man in the next bed.
He was asleep. She rang for the nurse. When the nurse arrived,
my mom asked her if she would find the music and have it
turned down. The nurse paused, then said that she did not hear
any music and diplomatically suggested that maybe the oxygen
machines were making odd noises. My mom did not press the
issue but knew from two years of listening to oxygen machines
that they do not sing.

She sat down beside Dad, listening to the choral music.
From his semi-prone position, Dad raised his head, looked
straight ahead, and said in a strong, young man voice, "Who is

that standing at the end of my bed?" His eyes stared as if he could not believe what he was seeing. Mom was placatory, told him that the nurse had been in. He would have none of it. His grin was ear to ear. He repeated, "Who is that standing at the end of my bed?"

Shortly after, my mom noticed that he was not breathing. The doctor said that he'd had a small heart attack . . . the natural consequence of hypoxia. His death was pronounced.

She sat, waiting for relatives to arrive. She queried the doctor about eye movement under his lids, about what she thought were small muscle movements. The doctor assured her that after the heart stops, there may be reactive quivers. I was glad that she was there to wait while his spark calmed the quivers on their way.

The excitement and welcome he experienced while dying lent credence to all I have heard about the collective unconscious or the communion of saints. Souls with similar energy come with light and vast peace. They come from eons past. My mother's experience strengthened my belief that those who have touched my mind and heart—the Magdal-eder, Sophia, Emily, Rilke, Merton, and many other members from the frequency of my vibe family—will come for me.

The experience with my father's dying tempered everyone's uneasiness. Now when I consider being called back, whether the summons is sudden or anticipated . . . I have confidence that all will be well.

April 23, 1886

COMFORT PEEKS FROM THE END OF A SUNNY TUNNEL. I HEAR
neighborly talk, cutlery clatters, and dishes rattle a boney china
conversation. I see dust motes floating over me while a soft bed
supports me. I am deliciously aware of each detail, teeming with
calm. Floorboards creak, flies bounce off window glass, the linens
rasp dryly against my skin—in the midst of this, the sunny tunnel
holds my still-beating heart.

My breath becomes a zephyr sighed to anoint linen fibers. It
slips to my writing table where it collects a few scattered thoughts
leaked by my pen at last use. Then breathes itself over the floor to
the window and out to add itself to the airy swell passing by on
its way to the garden leaves and blooms. It sifts their scent and
creeps on through nearby gardens, preferring a friendly blending
with spring bloom than the stagnant stillness of a sick room.

On my zephyr goes, a breath touching everything in
its path—with far more familiarity than I ever would. My
imagination follows it. My zephyr bumps a tree and is pushed
up by a coolness of roots and damp grass. It is tickled by bark
toeholds that let it skip to leaves that finally shoo it on to join
the air of all. A thin shawl of sky is no barrier as blue fades into
a wary gray warning of deepening to a dark black, velvet zone of
gifts that ease breath back to light. Soon the many favors of earth
will propel me to light and keep me.

I will not want to stay here—the sunny tunnel will insist
with warm fervor—how lovely to pass through and learn only

through love—be consoled by all that has ever been. No doubt fragments of experience will follow me. They will come along and touch me like kisses. I tried to fix their sweetness or sting on paper in life—their furtive vigor could never be quite so neatly contained—but essences—the kisses—carry me through to be enfolded in glorious embrace.

I have not lived in vain. My spirit so easily quelled on earth suffers no such constraint in tunnel environs. I sip nectar beyond, suspended in adoration—the welcomers' steadfast anticipation unfurls—calling me back—any moment now—completion.

May 28, 2008

Dearest Em, how clearly you saw your sunny tunnel with its whisper of beginnings. My place is still one of seeking, groping at midpoint to find safe passage from my current well. I climb out covered with scratches of wisdom, to rest on a bright plateau and gather strength until the plateau reveals itself to be the bottom of a new well. In the climb through confusion, I see darkly, my fingertips feeling intuitively for hand-holds. There are many wells and less vision in these vertical tunnels.

Brick by ragged brick, I have inched from the well of my mother's well-intentioned but damaging presence—the well of my father's indifference—the well of isolation—the well of relationship projections—well after well. Each out-crawling does, in fact, find me bravely bearing abrasions of consciousness. Eager for the static calm of a lull. Eager eventually becomes ordinary, becomes a grave-like enclosure that forces me to face uncertainty again. If I engage, a well will show me well-worn rungs of reflection that are a way out.

My life has been a series of demi-deaths as this out-crawling cycle repeats. It's akin to Elizabeth Bishop's exhortation to lose something every day. She suggests that we would all do well to treat loss as something to master, not a disaster. She understood losing an attachment after its utility ceased, in preference for new attachments growing from the circumference around me. The folly of entrapment by outgrown bonds is apparent to people like me and Bishop who invested in the life of the mind rather than its rotting and rust-bound material counterparts.

Nonetheless, memory of loss hangs around, shoe-boxed on mental shelves, gifts from the wells. Shrunken strips of girlhood gone by. Years read away. Words that occupied time and provided distraction before they split into space leaving me with sketchy threads of story residue.

Also, shoe-boxed is the angst of adolescence, my first attempt at higher-ed, several churches, a country, jobs, a marriage, and motherhood memories. All examined, then shelved to shift my focus from potential significance to the present moment.

I pushed along in the belief that purpose was just ahead—if I stayed on the move so as to not feel the fright and necessity of hiding my breathing body—if I stayed with the belief that I could be free of the last glass shards that separated me from myself and the world. If I found the shards and ground them to powder. Or so I thought before I discovered that they would dissolve on their own in proportion to my ability to value myself.

A phenomenal turning point occurred in a wise therapist's office when I was thirty-seven years old. It was the day before Thanksgiving. I sat on her couch. She sat opposite. We mulled over my seemingly chronic detachment, my sense of disconnection. My mild dysphoria. My isolation. She got up from her chair to get a book from a nearby shelf. As I sat, hunched forward, space-time altered. With my eyes closed, I said, "I can see her! I can see her!" From across the room, the therapist asked, "Who can you see?"

She came over, sat down listening, while I described what I saw. I saw a spotlight shining on two figures set in a softly filtered gray-black space. One figure was a man wearing a charcoal-colored suit, dark tie, and bright white shirt. His head was an indistinct shadow against the dusky beyond, outside the spotlight. This man was holding the other figure—a beaming, three-year-old me. I wore a frothy dress of pink and white lace. I had lacy white socks that looked like clouds around my ankles in shiny black shoes. Such finery was nonexistent in my actual life at age three. The sides of my thin, fine, honey-colored hair had been twisted into two kiss-curls bumpy with marks left by bobby pins. Much too short bangs fringed my wide forehead. But the girl was me. Definitely me. And my grin. It was huge. My even, pearl-size baby teeth could not have been more exposed. I perched gladly in this man's arms. I had the impression that he had been taking care of me. I 'knew' that it was time now for him to return what he had guarded for more than thirty years.

The wise therapist recognized and validated my experience as a healthy breakthrough and not as evidence of a pathologically dissociated personality. Her grin was almost as large as my own. This experience was a major step in the reweaving of my raveled consciousness. During prior visits we had discussed my ability, which she called nothing short of brilliant, to go back inside my head and connect—with energy, with archetypes, with angels? To me, at those times it felt like a door opened in my brain. I looked and would 'know' something new. That day, she cheered my description and entered the excitement and peace with me. We were both changed.

Months of light followed. I was an embodiment of T.S. Eliot's image of returning to a place and knowing it for the first time. Each day of feeling—safe, responsive, noticing details— became part of a long series of firsts. From that moment in the therapist's office, living was less about hiding and more about belonging. Consciousness, with a sly and still shy invasive sense of value, had arrived.

Progress was steady, if slow since I had much to relearn. How to concentrate. How to finish things. How to hear and see. How to read a book and remember the story. How to remember conversation. How to permit small treats for myself. While praise and value may never be my defaults, now I know where to find them when unusual stress or tiredness triggers a temporary retreat from the moment.

Since that triumphant visit, I have had cycles of recollection—of the facts of my history, over which I had little control. Cycles of reconciling—to reigning circumstances. Cycles of reconnecting—with people and events from a baseline of worthiness. The wells have transformed into a vine of luxuriant bloom that creeps tenaciously with color to soften the hard trellis of my life.

And Emily, here we are together—years of rowing in Eden—done with the compass—done with the chart—our hearts are in port. Moored in port—our present.

From the grace-filled vibrancy of our space and time shifts, a fanciful image fuels forward movement. I feel like I am lolloping along in a cartoon car with one big wheel out of sync with the others. Inelegant progress—but progress. I see myself willing to develop a public life with depth equal to that of my private life. Movement by mini-completions toward the beginning where my sunny tunnel ends.